WORKING ACROSS
BOUNDARIES

WORKING

ACROSS

BOUNDARIES

PEOPLE, NATURE, AND REGIONS

Matthew J. McKinney

Shawn Johnson

LINCOLN INSTITUTE
OF LAND POLICY
CAMBRIDGE, MASSACHUSETTS

Library of Congress Cataloging-in-Publication Data

McKinney, Matthew.
   Working across boundaries : people, nature, and regions / Matthew J.
McKinney, Shawn Johnson.
      p. cm.
   Includes bibliographical references and index.
   ISBN 978-1-55844-191-0
   1. Regional planning--Political aspects. 2. Land use--Planning.
3. Natural resources--Co-management. I. Johnson, Shawn, 1974-
II. Lincoln Institute of Land Policy. III. Title.
   HT391.M3955 2009
   307.1--dc22
                           2009027444

Designed by Peter M. Blaiwas/Vern Associates, Inc., Newburyport, MA

Composed in Chaparral. Printed and bound by Puritan Press, in Hollis, New Hampshire.
The text paper is Rolland Enviro100, an acid-free, 100 percent recycled PCW sheet.

MANUFACTURED IN THE UNITED STATES OF AMERICA

Dedication

I dedicate this book to the two people who have most influenced my thinking about regional governance.

The first is John Parr, who passed away in 2007. I met John in 1979, when he was working for Colorado Governor Richard Lamm to facilitate a regional, multijurisdictional land use plan along the Front Range. Although a plan never emerged, this initiative demonstrated John's vision of the need to work across boundaries to provide cost-effective public services, manage urban growth, preserve agricultural lands and open space, and promote a sense of place and belonging.

The second person is Charles H. W. Foster, whom I met in 1990 at a workshop on the interstate management of the Missouri River. By this time, Henry had dedicated nearly 40 years to studying, creating, managing, and evaluating regional institutions for natural resource and environmental management. His breadth of experience and down-to-earth pragmatism captivated me. Like John, he encouraged me to find opportunities to help people think and act regionally, experiment with a diversity of approaches in bringing people together, and document the experiences.

I hope this book in some way reflects the profound influence that John and Henry have had on my professional life.

—Matthew J. McKinney
Helena, Montana

CONTENTS

Illustrations

Foreword

This work on regional collaboration grows out of what has itself become a long-standing collaboration between the Lincoln Institute of Land Policy and the University of Montana Center for Natural Resources and Environmental Policy (formerly the Public Policy Research Institute). Regional planning at different scales, territorial spillovers, and multijurisdictional governance has long been part of the Department of Planning and Urban Form's research and training agenda. Through a joint venture partnership, we have been able to study and field test the ideas in this book over nearly a decade, primarily through training sessions and place-based clinics on regional efforts that we held with Matt McKinney and his team at sites across North America. In addition to this volume, we have established a subcenter on the Lincoln Institute of Land Policy Web site that draws on this research and experience.

Although its first chapter answers the question, Why work across boundaries?, this book is really more about the how of regional collaboration than the why. That is appropriate, as it is intended for citizens, practitioners, and policy makers grappling with the challenges presented by transboundary issues who seek guidance on the process by which regional solutions can be identified and implemented. For them, the why is clear enough: complex regional issues and gaps in governance that occur when jurisdictions are unable to make effective decisions or take action to resolve problems.

The book presents an array of practical and tested strategies and techniques that can be employed across the range of land use, natural resource, and environmental issues at scales ranging from metropolitan to megaregional, including watersheds and ecosystems. Whether you are deeply engaged in a regional initiative, or just beginning to explore a regional strategy, this book can serve as the "missing manual." It provides ten guiding principles, five key questions for regional governance, and seven habits of effective implementation that can be referred to before, during, and after undertaking regional collaboration. I call particular attention to chapter 7 on evaluation, which can help in determining whether a regional initiative is working and whether it should be continued.

Although this is not a book of theory, it is worth noting that regional collaboration as presented here draws heavily on consensus building, which is itself based on the theory of mutual gains negotiation. In a sense, regional collaboration is about consensus building in space, and some of the approaches and terminology will be familiar to those trained in consensus building, mediation, negotiation, and related areas of practice. One shared insight from theory is that these processes, to be sustained, need to fulfill an expectation that the benefits to participating stakeholders will exceed the costs. In the long run, regional efforts need to be measured by regional results.

The spatial component makes this process interesting to many of us, but also helps to explain why regional collaboration can appear bewilderingly complex and difficult. We often deal with diverse stakeholders and conflicting interests that play out across complicated geographies. One case study that runs the gamut of regional land use, natural resource, and environmental issues is Calgary, Alberta, Canada, described in chapter 1. Calgary is at the core of a metropolitan region of 19 municipalities struggling with serious urban/suburban conflicts over rapid growth, including water supply and wastewater issues, played out in a landscape of massive resource extraction (oil sands) and important habitat for moose, bear, and beaver.

Having been involved in the regional consensus processes that ultimately led to the creation of the Barnstable County Assembly of Delegates, an elected legislative body, and passage of the Cape Cod Commission Act by the Massachusetts legislature, I can say from experience that the path from regional insight to regional action is not always easy or short. In the case of the commission, which was at the heart of a new regional planning and regulatory system, it took five years from conception to execution, and required extensive public engagement and formal acceptance by voters following an elaborate visioning process. Although the result would be categorized by this book in the strict compliance family of regional governance models, I like to think that all of those evening meetings led to a more democratic and friendly, albeit legislatively mandated, institution.

I tip my hat to Matt McKinney and his team for so concisely bringing together the rich learning and experience of many fellow practitioners in the regional arts and sciences. For those of you who have chosen to respond to the challenge of activating the potential that is locked up in your regions, may this book serve you well.

—Armando Carbonell
  Chairman
  Department of Planning and Urban Form
  Lincoln Institute of Land Policy

Acknowledgments

This book is the product of collaboration. The Lincoln Institute of Land Policy supported the research and writing of the book, and allowed my colleagues and me to undertake a series of regional collaboration clinics. These clinics allowed us to add value to local efforts and to develop and refine our thinking about regional collaboration.

Special thanks go to Armando Carbonell and Lisa Cloutier of the Institute's Department of Planning and Urban Form for their ongoing commitment and support; Peter Pollock, Ronald Smith Fellow of the Lincoln Institute, who reviewed countless drafts of the manuscript; and Ann LeRoyer, director of publications, who masterfully edited the manuscript and brought it to life.

Many of the lessons and practical strategies presented in this book emerged from our on-the-ground work with citizens and leaders in multiple regions throughout North America. We appreciate the opportunity to work with these pioneers, and hope this book celebrates and reflects their hard work.

I thank many colleagues who reviewed earlier drafts of the manuscript over the past few years, including Todd Bryan, Tom Christoffel, Bill Dodge, Pat Field, Henry Foster, George Frederickson, Malka Kopell, Cameron Moore, John Parr, Doug Porter, Michael Quinn, Ethan Seltzer, Ken Snyder, and Ron Thomas. I would also like to acknowledge the graduate students in the University of Montana's Natural Resources Conflict Resolution Program who consistently challenged our thinking on this topic and compelled us to sharpen our presentation.

Finally, I acknowledge the dedicated work of our team at the University of Montana Center for National Resources and Environmental Policy (formerly the Public Policy Research Institute). Shawn Johnson conducted research, organized and convened regional workshops, and helped write significant chunks of the original manuscript. Will Harmon refined that manuscript into a compelling narrative. Sarah Bates, Sheila Hoffland, and Daisy Patterson provided research and administrative support, and gracefully took care of innumerable pesky details.

Chapter 1

WHY WORK ACROSS BOUNDARIES?

B oundaries are ubiquitous features of civilization. People use them to distinguish one nation—or one backyard—from the next. Boundaries bring the world down to a manageable scale. Most landscapes are overlaid with patchworks of many boundaries, creating myriad jurisdictions at every level, from property lots to villages, towns, cities, and counties, up to states, provinces, nations, and international blocs. Add to those all the landholdings or management responsibilities of various public agencies, nonprofit groups, and private property owners, and the map quickly becomes a finely diced jigsaw puzzle of kingdoms large and small.

Generally, people are happy to work within the boundaries they have created for themselves. With no boundaries, we would not know where our responsibilities begin and end. Clean lines on a map solve that problem for many professionals and practitioners—a city planner knows the limit of her duties; a forest ranger knows precisely how far to range; and a state governor knows the physical extent over which he governs. Drawing a boundary around our work helps us focus and also prevents our jobs from expanding to fill all available time and energy.

But increasingly we are finding that we may have diced up our world to such a fine degree that the subsequent jurisdictions are often too small or too constrained in purpose to meet larger challenges and opportunities. A host of issues routinely transcends our elaborate grid of boundaries. Air pollution wafts across continents and oceans. Water carries contaminants downhill. Many wildlife species routinely cross imaginary lines to reach habitats and migration corridors. Invasive plants and animals move from homelands to new frontiers. Drought and wildfire can threaten whole landscapes.

Even our cities are not immune to such transboundary concerns. Planners and decision makers grapple with transportation, job markets, health care, crime, and other issues that do not stop at geopolitical boundaries. Such issues should make us smarter. They remind us that we are interdependent, tethered to our neighbors. They reveal that no single jurisdiction can effectively address every challenge on its own. In short, transboundary concerns reveal gaps in our strategies for governing and making decisions on natural resource and environmental issues.

When people work together across boundaries, they take part in something larger than their individual jurisdictions. They begin to function more or less as a region. Most people think of a region as a place tied together by topographic features—New England, the Great Lakes, or the Colorado Plateau. But regions are also places where people share a common understanding of their built and natural environments. Regional landscapes may be metropolitan, rural, undeveloped, or some mix of these. Regional collaboration, then, is working together on a scale that transcends the usual jurisdictional boundaries.

This is the sense of region that informs this book: a landscape that encompasses a given challenge or opportunity and that fits people's sense of identity and purpose.

THE PROBLEM: A GAP IN GOVERNANCE

Increasingly, the territory of the land use, natural resource, and environmental issues we face transcends the legal and geographic reach of existing jurisdictions and institutions. The people affected by this spatial mismatch have interdependent interests, which means that none of them has sufficient power or authority to address the problems adequately on their own. This creates a gap in governance—no single entity has the power or authority to address these types of transboundary issues, so there is a need to create informal and formal ways to work across boundaries.

What do we mean by the term *governance*? For starters, governance differs from government. Government occurs when people with formal, legal authority make plans and take action. In contrast, governance is what happens when citizens and groups (often including government agency officials) work together to plan and act based on their shared goals. Such efforts may or may not have formal authority or power (Blomgren Bingham, Nabatchi, and O'Leary 2005). If government is our elected representatives and experts at work, then governance is the people at work—citizens taking part in planning, decision making, and implementation. In short, governance is a transparent, public process that engages diverse interests through inclusive, informed, and deliberative dialogue and action.

The governance gap exists because no adequate forum or mechanism exists within government or through existing entities to address trans-boundary issues. Merely applying scientific or technical knowledge to address economic, social, or environmental concerns cannot close this gap. Nor is closing the gap simply about managing land more effectively and efficiently. At its core, working across boundaries is a sociopolitical challenge. It is a question of how people can integrate the interests and concerns of multiple jurisdictions, government agencies, and public and private stakeholders to address land use and other regional issues.

TYPES OF RESPONSES: THE CASE OF CALGARY

Life in the Calgary region in the province of Alberta, Canada, aptly illustrates the nature of regional issues and how people can work to close the governance gap (figure 1.1). The City of Calgary and its 18 neighboring municipalities are among the fastest growing areas in North America (Hope

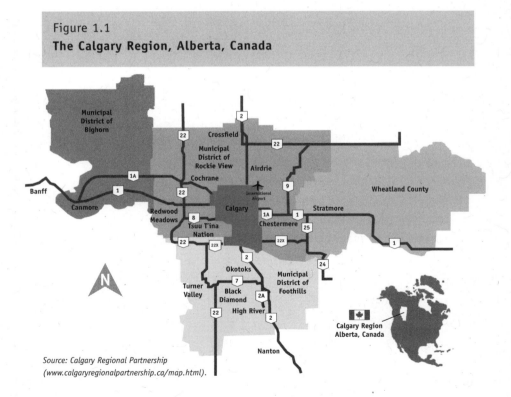

Figure 1.1
The Calgary Region, Alberta, Canada

Source: Calgary Regional Partnership
(www.calgaryregionalpartnership.ca/map.html).

2007). Between 2001 and 2006, Calgary's population increased by 12.4 percent, 84,000 new homes were built in the region, and 162,795 homes changed hands. Housing prices increased more than 40 percent in 2006 compared to 2005. Jobs in the goods-producing sector soared 21 percent in 2006, the most ever for a city in Canada, and the average earnings in Calgary jumped 19 percent between 2006 and 2008.

The primary driver of this growth is energy development, specifically the rich oil sands along the eastern front of the Canadian Rockies. These oil sands represent the world's largest proven petroleum reserves outside Saudi Arabia and cover an area larger than the state of Florida. The area is home to moose, bear, and beaver that inhabit the watery woodlands where oil is locked in the tarry soil. The energy industry estimates that enough oil can be economically extracted to fill Canada's needs for three centuries (Al-Qudsi 2005). With United States demand for Canadian crude oil forecast to double within eight years, investment in Alberta's oil sands began to snowball in 2007 and continues to grow (Schmidt 2007). Investment in oil sands has surged from $5.2 billion in 2003, when oil prices began to climb, to $16.1 billion in 2007, the latest year for which figures are available.

While growth in the Calgary region creates enormous opportunities for economic prosperity, it is also generating a number of challenges in managing the built and natural environments. A recent report prepared for the Calgary Citizen's Forum (Couroux et al. 2006) asserts that current growth patterns:

- promote and support sprawling, automobile-dependent development;
- increase reliance on fossil fuels and their impact on climate;
- create a loss of wildlife habitat and greenspace;
- deplete and degrade water resources;
- diminish the capacity of the region's infrastructure and social services;
- increase disease, premature death, and health care costs; and
- magnify social inequities and the loss of community.

These and similar concerns were cited by nearly one hundred elected officials and other people interviewed in 2006 by the Consensus Building Institute and the University of Montana's Public Policy Research Institute as part of an assessment of the Calgary region's response to ongoing pressures from growth and development (McKinney, Field, and Johnson 2007). One of the primary conclusions of this assessment was that working across boundaries would improve the ability of citizens and government officials to respond to both the positive and negative consequences of growth in the region. Consider the two following examples regarding water resources and economies of scale.

When the Municipal District of Rocky View proposed the development of a shopping center and horse racetrack in 2006, it approached its neighbor—the City of Calgary—to supply the necessary water. The city, which owns most of the water licenses on the nearby Bow River, declined the request. A moratorium on new water licenses from local rivers then compelled Rocky View to look north to the Red Deer River. Instead of building a three-kilometer water line from a city hook-up, Rocky View was forced to consider a sixty-two-kilometer line from the Red Deer River at a cost of more than $40 million.

As the population in the Calgary region continues to surge, neighboring communities are likely to face similar water-supply issues. Although studies show that the region has enough water to meet its projected growth needs until 2075, the supply depends in large part on the City of Calgary's licenses for the Bow and Elbow rivers. During interviews conducted by researchers at the Consensus Building Institute and the University of Montana, Calgary officials said that they are willing to share the city's water supply only if future development in surrounding jurisdictions is tied to a regional land use plan. Clearly, Calgary wields significant power, yet no single jurisdiction can solve water-supply or growth issues on its own. The fiscal impacts of uncoordinated growth are high, which seems to be steering jurisdictions away from competition and toward cooperation, especially with regard to basic resources such as water.

In the second example, opportunities of scale may lure the 19 jurisdictions in the Calgary region into working across the boundaries that separate them. A recent study suggests that these communities can best satisfy their individual demands for wastewater services by creating one or more "regional" facilities (CH2MHILL 2007). The study analyzed social, economic, and environmental impacts and concluded that shared wastewater facilities would reduce costs in all three arenas. In short, by collaborating, regional partners can jointly seek out opportunities and economies of scale that are unavailable to jurisdictions acting on their own.

Concerns over transboundary issues in the Calgary region are not new. As early as 1951, the Alberta Provincial Government created the Calgary

Regional Planning Commission (CRPC) to develop and regulate land use in and around Calgary, including the municipal districts of Rocky View, Bighorn, and Foothills, and Wheatland County. CRPC wielded the power of subdivision approval, giving it complete control over development and conservation within the region. Such consolidation (called amalgamation in Canada) was occurring elsewhere in Alberta and throughout Canada, mandated from the province and often without asking for or obtaining local consent. In the Calgary region, some of the surrounding urban centers supported consolidation, and by 1964 Calgary had more than tripled in size (to 157 square miles). Significantly, consolidation occurred early enough in the city's development that it was not encumbered by preexisting, disparate planning institutions and cultures, as were nearly all other Canadian examples of consolidation.

While consolidation in the Calgary region apparently added value to the urban centers, neighboring rural municipal districts were much less supportive of those plans. When CRPC was granted the power of subdivision approval, rural municipalities felt condemned by a "biased, selfish, and prejudiced" system to be in a "powerless position" (Bettison, Kenward, and Taylor 1975). Consolidation also created an inequity in the distribution of the business tax base, since taxes were directed to the municipality that provided municipal services to the workers and families of a business (in this case the City of Calgary). As such, rural districts were denied revenue desperately needed for their own improvements. This inequality reinforced longstanding resentment on the part of the rural districts regarding their rights as landowners and the feeling that the rural municipalities were nothing but "land banks" frozen in anticipation of future urban expansion.

In short, rural communities around Calgary grew to feel that CRPC enabled the City of Calgary to impose its vision on others. CRPC and all other regional planning commissions across Alberta were eventually eliminated via the Municipal Government Act in 1995, which authorized local jurisdictions to develop intermunicipal development plans (IDPs) to address transboundary issues. Under this approach, which remains in force today, regional planning once again became contingent on voluntary, cooperative participation.

Under the Municipal Government Act, growth management and land use planning have not been as coordinated (or as regulated) as under the CRPC. Instead, individual municipalities have taken ownership for planning and development within their borders. Though numerous IDPs exist, they are mostly bilateral (between two adjacent jurisdictions) and are limited in scope and/or weak in their monitoring and enforcement provisions. The variation in growth pressures throughout the region has resulted in different policies and paradigms from one municipality to the next.

The most recent phase of regional governance in the Calgary region is represented by the Calgary Regional Partnership (CRP). This nonprofit organization emerged in 1999 under the guidance and leadership of elected officials in the 19 jurisdictions that compose the Calgary region. It provides a valuable forum or platform to share information, build relationships, and develop joint projects. After several years of developing a solid foundation, in 2006 CRP launched what many believe to be its most ambitious project to date: the creation of a regional land use plan. Originally, this project was referred to as the Regional Growth and Sustainability Framework, reflecting the overwhelming fear and resistance to the ideas of "land use" and "planning."

In early 2007, members of CRP unanimously adopted a regional vision and "Terms of Agreement for Working Together: A Commitment to Develop a Regional Land-Use Plan for the Calgary Region." Among other provisions, this agreement specifies the following points.

■ The regional land use plan shall be the comprehensive plan for land use and growth management in the region.
■ The plan shall acknowledge, respect, and uphold the autonomy of individual jurisdictions, while serving as a plan for land use and growth management throughout the region.
■ The plan shall not create another level of government or bureaucracy, but rather shall supplement the function and structure of all existing municipalities.
■ The plan shall represent the region's desire to capture the opportunities of coordinated regional growth planning, including environmental and socioeconomic balance and administrative and land use efficiency.

As of this writing, CRP is managing the process of developing and drafting a regional land use plan, which is scheduled for completion in 2009. Ongoing efforts to improve regional water, wastewater, and public transit systems are being integrated into the land use planning process. For example, in 2008 the Province of Alberta earmarked $2 billion for regional transportation projects in the Calgary area. CRP anticipates using at least a portion of these funds to improve the network of commuter bus service among outlying communities, and to use bus-based public transit to complement new heavy commuter and light rail projects throughout the region (Hope 2008).

The Calgary region's history of experiments in regional governance reflects trends throughout North America, and not just in fast-growing metropolitan areas. The governance gap—and ways to close it—plays out in many different land use, natural resource, and environmental arenas and at many different scales. Cities and their collar communities can clearly benefit from collaborating as a region. Based in part on the success of regional collaboration at the metropolitan and watershed scale, people are bringing these same concepts and practices to bear on ecosystems (such as the Florida Everglades, the intermountain Crown of the Continent, and habitat conservation plans) and megaregions (such as Cascadia in the Pacific Northwest or the Great Lakes in the Midwest).

THE FOCUS OF THIS BOOK

Practical experience—supported by research into many regional efforts in North America—suggests that there is no single model for closing the gap in governance created by transboundary issues. In fact, the best ways to fill the gap are homegrown, tailored to suit the issue at hand, and adapted to the unique needs and interests of each region. Based on this premise, this book presents an effective process to address land use issues that cut across boundaries. Presenting such a process is quite different from assessing existing policies or plans to deal with such problems, or even generating additional substantive prescriptions.

The distinction here between substance and process is not trivial. There is a huge difference between what should be done about a particular transboundary land use or water issue and how people who care about such issues should determine what ought to happen. The first problem is one of substance and the relative effectiveness of alternative policies and plans. The second is one of process—how to bring together the appropriate people with the best available information to address land-related issues that cut across multiple jurisdictions, sectors, and disciplines.

This book is a guide to improve the process of working across boundaries, which we call "regional collaboration." It presents a variety of principles, techniques, strategies, and concepts to help people diagnose regional problems, design an appropriate regional forum, develop and implement regional action plans, and evaluate and adapt their regional initiatives. We refer to these materials as "tools," not because of their technical complexity—most of the ideas are just organized common sense—but because of their emphasis on utility and their application to land use, natural resource, and environmental issues at several different scales, including metropolitan areas, watersheds, ecosystems, and megaregions. We offer these ideas and tools as a work in progress and look forward to your feedback on how to improve the emerging field of regional collaboration.

Chapter 2

CLOSING THE GOVERNANCE GAP

Regional transboundary issues reveal a gap in governance, although the scope and nature of that gap vary depending on the issues at hand. Some gaps are small—different groups working on the same spatially defined issue (such as conserving habitat for an endangered species), but unaware of each other's efforts. Other gaps are enormous and symptomatic of problems (such as climate change) that are simply too broad and deep for any existing jurisdiction to cope with on its own. Most gaps fall between these two extremes.

Not surprisingly, people have invented a variety of ways to close such gaps that are tailored to fit the scope and nature of their particular issue or situation. A small gap may need nothing more than a casual network to link a handful of previously isolated people or groups. Large gaps typically require a more formal and structured approach. Regardless of size and scope, however, these various ways to close the gap fall under the umbrella of regional collaboration. They tend to move through a similar four-stage cycle: diagnosing the situation, designing a process, taking action, and evaluating and adapting the process as needed. This cycle is explained in chapter 3, but first we examine the range of designs or models for closing the governance gap.

Based on our experience with regional collaboration and our study of the hundreds of regional initiatives in North America, we see a continuum of approaches—from informal networks, to more formal partnerships, to regional institutions (figure 2.1). Thinking in terms of this continuum helps to recognize that these approaches overlap in some ways, and that the differences among them are often subtle. Regional initiatives also tend to follow a progression from informal to more formal as people go through the process of thinking and acting regionally.

Figure 2.1
A Continuum of Regional Collaboration

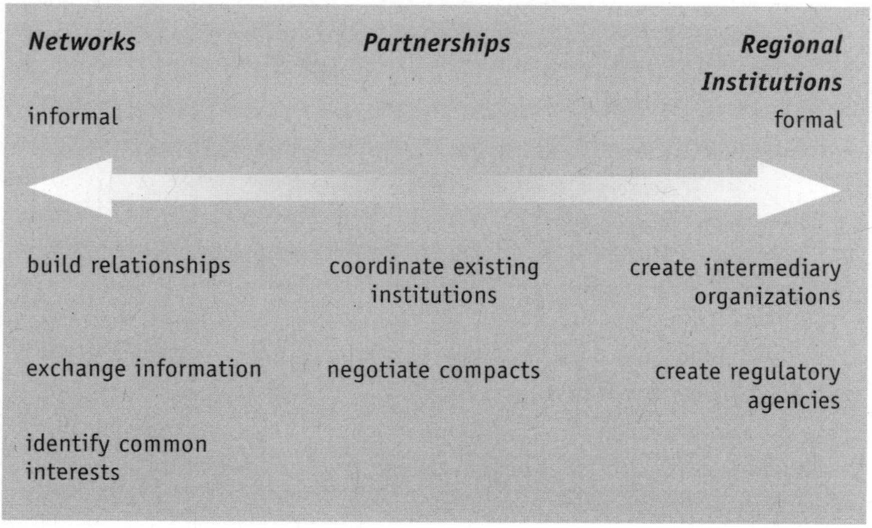

Networks	*Partnerships*	*Regional Institutions*
informal		formal

build relationships	coordinate existing institutions	create intermediary organizations
exchange information	negotiate compacts	create regulatory agencies
identify common interests		

The distinction between a network and a partnership, or a partnership and a regional institution, is not always clear and clean. These categories are intentionally broad, and within each are various models and approaches that also range from informal to formal. In a 2007 conversation with Douglas Porter, a recognized expert in land use and growth management, he suggested that:

> All regional efforts are assemblages of cooperating interests and groups, and all have established some type of working arrangement—some more artfully framed than others. The differences appear in aspects such as the range of issues and concerns that bring them together, the size and complexity of the geographical area they are focused on, the strength of the structural relationships they have established in which to function, the type of "official" establishment within recognized public or private organizations, and their method of assuring (or not) a continuing presence.

NETWORKS

A network is an informal arrangement where two or more people exchange ideas, build relationships, identify common interests, explore options on how to work together, share power, and solve problems of mutual interest—whether or not they have the formal authority to do so (Innes and Rongerude 2005; Mandell n.d.). Networks are "loosely linked autonomous players. . . . They [do] not function like hierarchical organizations with authority flowing from top to bottom. . . . Nor [do] they operate like advocacy organizations, whose members rally around a vision, leader, and a set of policies. Participants [are] independent and diverse; . . . they [share and coordinate], but in a different way from a bureaucratic or advocacy model" (Innes and Rongerude 2005, ix). Scholars studying network governance offer the following distinctions among terms (Keast et al. 2004).

- *Networking* refers to people making connections with each other by going to meetings and conferences, as well as through the use of communication technology such as email and web-based discussion groups.
- *Networks*, which involve networking, occur when links among a number of individuals and organizations become more formalized and sustained.
- *Network structures* emerge when people realize that they (and the organizations they represent) cannot solve a particular problem or issue by working independently and that the only way to achieve their interests is by actively working together.

The effectiveness of any networking arrangement hinges on the degree to which participants share a vision and whether some capacity exists (often embodied in one person or a small staff) to coordinate and convene activities among the independent players. A network functions when the players embrace a common vision, while acting unilaterally to achieve that vision.

Networks are often a useful strategy for responding to cyclical or sporadic issues, such as noxious weeds, drought, and wildfire. Some networks form around a constellation of issues. For example, the Chicagoland Environmental Network is a resource for anyone interested in nature or conservation-related activities in northeastern Illinois and surrounding areas. The network links more than two hundred organizations involved in habitat restoration; wetland, prairie, and watershed projects; urban gardening; energy conservation; composting; wildlife conservation; and recycling. People rely on the network for finding volunteer opportunities, job announcements, events, and information on each of the participating organizations. Such networks may evolve into more formal networking structures, such as the Stewardship Network in Michigan, as key players jointly acknowledge a need to collaborate over the long haul.

Participants applaud the ability of networks to build relationships, forge common visions, and solve some problems. Also, people who are leery of more formal approaches may be willing to participate in a network. Participants can choose the intensity and frequency of their involvement, and they may opt out (or in) as it suits them. Many people favor networking because it tends to be homegrown and bottom-up (rather than top-down). Where more formal models such as partnerships and institutions may be seen as another (possibly unwanted) layer of government, networks can be a more palatable option for citizens and government officials alike (box 2.1).

PARTNERSHIPS

In contrast to networks, where commitments tend to be open-ended, a partnership is a somewhat more formal relationship between two or more entities wherein each accepts responsibility to contribute a specified, not necessarily equal, level of effort to achieve a common goal. The objectives of regional partnerships may initially be exchanging ideas and identifying common interests (similar to networks), but typically they move in the direction of sharing resources, working on common problems, and delivering specific types of services (e.g., water, wastewater treatment, parks and recreation, economic development). Partnerships may form among government agencies, nongovernmental organizations, or a mix of both.

In the context of regional land use, the United States is home to more than 450 regional partnerships in the form of councils of governments (COGs), metropolitan planning organizations (MPOs), and other types of intergovernmental agreements. As a general rule, these partnerships do not have the authority to make and impose decisions, but are designed to foster regional cooperation and improve delivery of services (National Association of Regional Councils 2008). Even without formal regulatory and oversight authority, these regional partnerships (particularly MPOs) often succeed at influencing and facilitating regional collaboration because of their ability to direct federal funding for transportation and infrastruc-

Box 2.1
Strengths and Weaknesses of Networks

Strengths

- Typically require less time, money, and other resources than partnerships or regional institutions
- Well suited to responding to urgent problems
- Minimizes administrative and bureaucratic hurdles
- Can be built on existing relationships
- Can be readily scaled to the issue and potential solutions at hand

Weaknesses

- May be difficult to sustain due to lack of formal structure
- Lack of specific, formal agreement on roles and responsibilities can lead to misunderstanding and friction
- In contentious situations, the necessary trust among participants may be difficult to forge or sustain
- Highly susceptible to changes in power, politics, personnel, and resources (Networks function at the level of interpersonal relationships so are only as effective as those relationships.)
- Can be challenging to distribute costs and benefits equitably among players in the network
- Tools and resources (and perhaps even the spirit of cooperation) may disappear when the issue that spawned the network goes away

Source: Parr, Riehm, and McFarland (2006).

ture projects toward those projects that align with a regional vision and set of goals (Lincoln Institute of Land Policy 2009).

In the water resources arena, partnerships formed around interjurisdictional watersheds and rivers often take the form of a compact—a voluntary but binding agreement that often becomes part of the laws of the participating jurisdictions. The Colorado River Basin Compact, completed in 1922, represents the first use of a compact to allocate and manage water among multiple states. Other multistate and regional compacts have since formed, notably around the Arkansas, Cumberland, Delaware, Klamath, Rio Grande, St. Lawrence, and Susquehanna river basins (Lincoln Institute of Land Policy 2009).

Among the array of partnerships, three models predominate in the land use arena: regional councils, intergovernmental agreements, and intergovernmental consolidations. These models are presented from the least structured and least controversial to the most structured, most controversial, and most difficult to implement (box 2.2).

REGIONAL COUNCILS: COORDINATING EXISTING AGENCIES ■
According to the National Association of Regional Councils (2008),

> A regional council is a multi-service entity with state and locally defined boundaries that delivers a variety of federal, state, and local programs while continuing its function as a planning organization, technical assistance provider, and "visionary" to its member local governments. As such, they are accountable to local units of government and effective partners for state and federal governments.

Of the 39,000 local, general purpose governments in the United States (counties, cities, townships, towns, villages, boroughs), more than 35,000 are served by regional councils.

The Puget Sound Regional Council (PSRC) is a good example of this type of regional partnership (Dempsey, Goetz, and Larson 2000). Building on previous coordination among local governments, the PSRC was formed in 1991 as an inclusive association of cities, towns, counties, port authorities, and state agencies. The council serves as a forum for developing policies and making decisions about regional growth and transportation issues in the four-county central Puget Sound region. The participating agencies each play their role in working toward the common goals of VISION 2020, an overarching vision for directing growth into urban areas and regional growth centers in an environmentally responsible way, fostering economic development, and providing efficient transportation.

Regional councils are valuable because they provide an ongoing forum for local governments and others to build agreement and work through conflicts on shared issues. Once they establish relationships and a bit of momentum or a track record of success, they are able to respond to new and emergent regional issues. They also create efficiencies by sharing resources and jointly solving problems that no single agency or jurisdiction could resolve alone.

The effectiveness of regional councils, however, depends on their ability to build consensus across a broad spectrum of interests. Since they have

Box 2.2
Strengths and Weaknesses of Partnerships

Strengths

- Create more or less permanent forums to facilitate regional thinking and action
- Allow government agencies to work across boundaries either within existing government structures or by realigning functions
- Provide flexibility to include representatives from all sectors—public, private, nonprofit, university, etc.
- Clarify roles and responsibilities, thereby minimizing misunderstanding and friction among participants
- May ensure implementation by creating the right incentives and/or binding agreements

Weaknesses

- Authority may be limited to planning and visioning, not implementation
- Effectiveness depends on good-faith efforts and continuity of participation among individuals in each agency; staff turnover can derail group efforts
- Equitably distributing costs and benefits among participants can be challenging
- Individual partners may want their interests to predominate, making it difficult to equitably prioritize projects despite widespread agreement on a regional vision

little to no authority to take action, implementation depends on the good will and cooperation of the participants. Serious disagreement on an issue or proposed solution makes it very difficult to effect change. Even when there is consensus on an issue, there are no guarantees that every participant will effectively implement an agreed-upon recommendation.

A regional council is more likely to be effective when people in the region share a profound sense of place and regional identity, which enables them to rally around a common regional vision. Collaborative civic leadership is also crucial. Such leadership, in turn, invites broad, inclusive citizen participation.

INTERGOVERNMENTAL AGREEMENTS: SHAPING A COMMON AGENDA ■ One way to overcome the limitations of regional councils and rally disparate jurisdictions around a common agenda is to negotiate agreements among the various agencies involved. Such agreements can be either binding or nonbinding.

Intergovernmental agreements (IGAs) are quite common among neighboring jurisdictions, whether they be adjoining communities or land and resource managing agencies. For example, many towns and cities enter into contracts or joint service agreements to increase efficiencies and reduce costs for services such as law enforcement, fire fighting, water supply and treatment, and garbage collection. Land and resource agencies also enter into IGAs to streamline services, but more often the motivation is to coordinate management of the land or resource itself. Such an IGA may enable two or more agencies to protect contiguous wildlife habitat or migration corridors, for example.

As in river basins, the term *compact* is sometimes used for binding agreements among many jurisdictions. A compact commits the jurisdictions to shape their individual plans and management actions to fit within the larger regional agenda outlined in the agreement. Some metropolitan areas bring all the local jurisdictions together under an IGA or compact to meet requirements and obtain federal funding. For example, in the greater Denver metropolitan area, some 44 municipalities and other jurisdictions have signed on to the Mile High Compact, which recognizes Metro Vision 2020 as the regional framework for managing growth and development. Under the compact, each jurisdiction's comprehensive plan must conform to the overarching goals and policies of Metro Vision 2020. Local jurisdictions buy in to the regional vision because they helped draft it.

The strength of an IGA is that it is voluntary and binding—at least most of the time. Given that parties to the negotiated agreement define the terms and conditions of the IGA, they are more likely to follow through and implement the agreed-upon provisions. IGAs typically clarify roles and responsibilities as well, thereby minimizing the chance of misunderstanding and friction. Like networks and other types of partnerships, IGAs can also be adapted to the unique needs and interests of a particular region. While IGAs may require additional staff and budget to implement and may be difficult to revise and restructure in the face of changing circumstances, these issues can typically be addressed during the negotiation of the IGA.

INTERGOVERNMENTAL CONSOLIDATIONS: MERGING FUNCTIONS ■

Short of establishing a new regional institution, a more permanent type of partnership is to merge or consolidate functions. Again, this approach is most common in metropolitan areas. In the United States, there are more than 30 city-county consolidations or mergers. Some smaller communities have consolidated to make the most of limited budgets, but larger cities also merge with adjoining communities and counties. Notable consolidated metropolitan areas include New Orleans (1805), Boston (1821), Philadelphia (1854), San Francisco (1856), New York City (1898), Denver (1902), Honolulu (1907), Jacksonville (1968), Anchorage (1975), and Louisville (2003). In Canada, municipal restructuring, often driven by provincial governments, has resulted in consolidation (or amalgamation) at large scales, too, including Toronto in 1998 (affecting roughly 2.5 million citizens), Ottawa in 2001 (600,000 citizens), and Montreal in 2002 (2 million citizens) (Kitchen 2003).

The advantage of merging or consolidating multiple (fragmented) functions into a coherent partnership is that—at least in theory—it will create a more effective and efficient approach to the regional problem at hand. Proponents often cite potential economies of scale and reduced costs. Not all consolidations are aimed at cutting costs, however. The merger of Louisville and Jefferson County, Kentucky, is notable because it was motivated primarily by the region's concern about enhancing its stature. When voters approved the merger in 2003, the Greater Louisville region climbed overnight in population ranks from 65th to an estimated 23rd largest in the nation. This move led to enhanced revenue streams and improvements in emergency services and stormwater drainage systems and a streamlined construction permitting process.

The downside of consolidation is that it typically requires much political capital and is often opposed by one or more jurisdictions. When a few communities in an area resist consolidation, the region remains fragmented.

REGIONAL INSTITUTIONS

Continuing along the spectrum from networks and partnerships, the most formal, structured response to transboundary issues is the creation of new institutions that function at the regional scale and can span a range of activities from advisory to regulatory. At one end, some may serve as intermediary organizations that help convene and coordinate other players in the region. Others provide technical assistance or serve as a vehicle for funding or as a clearinghouse for information. At the other end, such institutions may be agencies with regulatory authority over planning, land use, water, or other resources management.

INTERMEDIARY ORGANIZATIONS ■ When people in a region conclude that some type of ongoing organization is needed to promote and support regional thinking and action—in other words, where networks and partnerships are necessary but not sufficient—they have created what might be termed "intermediary organizations." These formal, usually nonprofit organizations play a number of intermediary roles, from catalyzing, convening, and coordinating, to advocating and conducting research.

Regional Plan Association (RPA), founded in 1922, is an independent nonprofit organization dedicated to improving the quality of life and the economic competitiveness of the 31-county New York–New Jersey–Connecticut region through research, planning, and advocacy. RPA has a tremendous record of accomplishments, beginning with the First Regional Plan (1929), which provided a blueprint for the existing transportation and open space networks. Now working to implement the Third Regional Plan, RPA is working with business leaders, communities, public agencies, and others on issues ranging from transportation and open space to community design, the workforce, and the economy.

On the West Coast, the Sierra Business Council (SBC) was created in 1994 to demonstrate that vibrant communities, fair and prosperous economies, and healthy ecosystems are not competing interests. On the contrary, when all three thrive, everyone wins. SBC includes over seven hundred member organizations. Like RPA, SBC has an impressive resume: an annual leadership institute to help build regional capacity; state of the region reports to track selected indicators of social, economic, and environmental health; and numerous partnerships at the local, regional, and state level to generate funding, knowledge, and capacity to foster green building, preserve open space, and respond to climate change.

In nearly every corner of the country, intermediary organizations are emerging to help fill the gap in governance and provide leadership on a mix of social, economic, and environmental issues. Some other notable organizations include Joint Venture: Silicon Valley Network (California), Great Valley Center (California), Envision Utah, Treasure Valley Partnership (Idaho), Cumberland Region Tomorrow (Tennessee), myregion.org (Florida), Calgary Regional Partnership, and Yellowstone Business Partnership (Wyoming, Idaho, and Montana).

Many of these organizations use research, information, and education to reach out to a broad diversity of people in their region, and to raise awareness, build trust, and identify common interests and shared goals. Accessibility and credibility are key ingredients for success in such an approach. From this foundation, the institution can create a compelling story line and begin to build strong working relationships among stakeholders. With no recourse to regulatory power, intermediary organizations tend to offer incentives for participation and compliance with the regional vision or agenda. Also, by sharing information and resources with government officials in the region, intermediary organizations can tie in to formal decision-making arenas. This is crucial for achieving on-the-ground results, particularly on land use issues.

Intermediary organizations provide a permanent vehicle to create a sense of regional identity, educate citizens and leaders, advocate for the region, and monitor progress. While they can sidestep shifts in political power and institutional preferences, and are often more flexible and adaptive to changing circumstance, such organizations do not have the authority to make binding policies or plans. As with partnerships, the effectiveness of intermediary organizations depends on their ability to forge consensus and persuade people to take action.

REGULATORY AGENCIES ■ Most intermediary organizations address regional issues through education and incentives. In some situations, however, that "carrot" approach is not enough to effect the desired change, so the "stick" of decision-making and regulatory authority must be used in its place.

Regional regulatory agencies exist at several different scales, from metropolitan to interstate. In both the Metropolitan Council in Minneapolis and St. Paul, Minnesota, and the Portland (Oregon) Metropolitan Council, the agency promulgates policies for land use, water quality, and open space (among other things) that must be followed by the affected cities and counties.

The Tahoe Regional Planning Agency, enacted by Congress in 1969, was the first interstate regional planning agency in the country (Strong 1984). Led by a 15-member governing board of local elected officials and appointees from California and Nevada, this agency is authorized to adopt environmental quality thresholds and enforce ordinances designed to achieve them.

The effectiveness of any regulatory agency revolves around several factors. Clearly, state and federal legislation creating and endorsing an agency provides outright legal authority and capacity without the procedural hurdles of coordinating multiple local jurisdictions. Even with such power, an agency will fight fewer battles and enjoy more support if it can create a friendly constituency within the region. In particular, it remains important for the agency to be inclusive of all interests, transparent in its decisions and actions, and responsive and adaptive to people's concerns.

Unlike networks and most partnerships, formal regional institutions—both intermediary organizations and regulatory agencies—provide a permanent vehicle to promote and support regional solutions to transboundary problems. They typically use incentives and disincentives for local jurisdictions to embrace and work toward regional goals. Some are bestowed with the legal authority to make binding decisions and enforce compliance. Such institutions can also play a sustained role in creating a strong sense of regional identity, educating citizens and leaders, advocating for the region, and monitoring progress.

Despite the advantages of new institutions, the suggestion to create one rarely receives a warm welcome. Existing local, state, and federal agencies may object to relinquishing any of their own authority or autonomy. Policy makers and citizens alike may be skeptical and averse to creating another layer of government. Proponents of this approach therefore must forge new political alliances, negotiate mutually beneficial arrangements among jurisdictions, and persuade naysayers. A good dose of timing and luck is also essential.

Further, new regional institutions require significant financial and human capital once they are established. According to the director of one such entity, they consume a great deal of effort to sustain themselves, given their bureaucratic nature, political volatility, and ambitious goals (box 2.3). For these and other reasons, the number of newly minted regional institutions remains limited (Calthorpe and Fulton 2001; Derthick 1974; Jensen 1965; Robbins, Frank, and Ross 1983).

OVERARCHING LESSONS

Several lessons emerge from these rich and diverse responses to regional, transboundary issues. The first lesson is that, regardless of the particular type of response—network, partnership, or regional institution—working across boundaries requires a willingness and ability to engage people and

Box 2.3
Strengths and Weaknesses of Regional Institutions

Strengths
- Create a permanent forum for addressing transboundary issues
- May have authority to implement and regulate land use decisions
- Provide a central avenue for integrating the interests and concerns of citizens and stakeholders
- May be better able to address long-term regional concerns, as they are not as susceptible to immediate political pressures

Weaknesses
- May not have authority to implement or regulate land use decisions
- Often have high start-up and maintenance costs
- May be politically beholden to regional, state, or federal entities at the expense of local interests and concerns
- Less adaptable to changing circumstances than networks or partnerships

organizations with diverse viewpoints and agendas, to create mutual-gain solutions that advance competing or divergent interests together rather than creating winners and losers, and to translate vision into actions.

Second, regional collaboration varies tremendously in terms of who leads the initiative as well as in scale, purpose, issues, activities, structure, funding, and time frame. While some initiatives augment existing government institutions, others are more ad hoc in nature, filling gaps in governance at varying scales. As the examples presented above suggest, regional collaboration can be and is applied at every level, from neighborhoods and municipalities, to counties, watersheds, and states, to multistate and multinational ecosystems and bioregions.

Third, regional collaboration produces a variety of outcomes including but not limited to fostering regional identity, building social and political capacity, taking action, and improving public policy. It often begins as an adjunct to politics as usual, but may end up fundamentally reconfiguring those politics. Whether formal or ad hoc, regional initiatives create public opportunities that would not otherwise exist to address issues that cut across multiple jurisdictions. They not only supplement other public processes, but represent new arenas for public decision making. This outcome is not only structural but also conceptual, and is as much a matter of culture and socialization as of skills and training.

Fourth, regional collaboration includes both a procedural element (how to plan or govern across boundaries) and a spatial element (how to think and act at the appropriate geographic scale). The procedural aspects of regional collaboration build on and synthesize theories of regional planning, multiparty negotiation, ecosystem management, multijurisdictional water management, political science, and bioregional philosophy. In general, the focus of the procedural element is on designing new systems of governance, both formal and informal, rather than preventing and/or resolving disputes per se. The spatial element of regional collaboration realizes the need to map problems, manage data from multiple jurisdictions and sectors, visualize alternative futures, and assess impact on a distinctly geographic basis. All of these activities create additional complexity in addressing regional, transboundary problems.

Finally, there is no single model for working across boundaries, but rather a set of principles, habits, or key ingredients for successful regional collaboration. Whether a region takes a formal or informal approach, these principles can be found at work in nearly all effective efforts. To be successful, regional collaboration must be homegrown—designed and built by those who best understand the region. In this respect, form follows function. The examples presented earlier illustrate that the form of regional collaboration varies depending on the specific needs and interests of each region. The underlying principles, however, remain the same.

A CLASSIC THEORY OF REGIONAL GOVERNANCE

In one of the most impassioned yet ignored theories of regional governance, John Wesley Powell, after surveying the American West in 1890, argued that the most appropriate institutions for governing western land and other natural resources are commonwealths defined by watersheds (figure 2.2). He reasoned that "there is a body of interdependent and unified interests and values, all collected in [a] hydrographic basin, and all segregated from the rest of the world by well-defined boundaries. The people in such a district have common interests, common rights, and common duties, and must necessarily work together for common purposes" (Powell

1890, 114). Powell's insights were largely ignored as the West was settled, but his reasoning underpins many of today's watershed councils, river basin groups, and other natural systems–based regional institutions.

Figure 2.2
Powell's Watershed Commonwealths

Chapter 3

A PRINCIPLED APPROACH TO REGIONAL COLLABORATION

A ny region's issues, interests, and circumstances are unique to that area, so no single model for collaboration works in every situation. The process of regional collaboration must be tailored to the needs of each region. That said, most regional efforts that achieve their goals share several common features. First, the collaborative process tends to be fluid and cyclical. Rather than following a rigid, linear, step-by-step sequence, regional collaboration often progresses in overlapping loops, with any number of activities occurring simultaneously. Second, this cycle includes four basic stages: diagnose, design, take action, and evaluate (figure 3.1).

Figure 3.1
The Cycle of Regional Collaboration

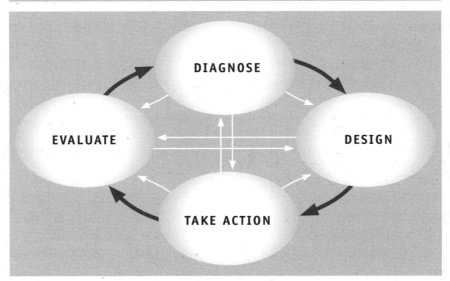

During the critical but often overlooked diagnosis stage, the goal is to determine the need to work across boundaries. Regional collaboration is not a panacea, and it is not appropriate in all situations. The best way to ensure that regional collaboration is used appropriately and effectively is to take time to consider whether and how to apply it to a particular situation. During design the goal is to match the process to the situation. Again, there is no single model of regional collaboration, so strategies and tools should be tailored to suit the unique needs and interests of the region. When taking action, the goal is to formulate and implement effective, appropriate actions that result in the desired outcomes. During evaluation the goal is to learn from the actions taken and to adapt the regional vision and strategy to improve its effectiveness.

Given the fluid nature of working across boundaries, circumstances routinely compel people to tackle various steps within two or more stages at once, or temporarily to skip forward or backward. Many regional efforts progress somewhat naturally from diagnosis to design to taking action to evaluation, but feedback loops occur at every stage, allowing people to pause and modify a previous stage, or to be proactive and anticipate problems or opportunities. This looping nature of working across boundaries reveals its strengths as a flexible, responsive, adaptive process.

A third common feature of effective regional collaboration is that the stages within the cycle are guided by a set of ten general principles.

Box 3.1
Ten Principles of Effective Regional Collaboration

Diagnose
1. Identify the compelling issue or catalyst.
2. Determine if there is a constituency for change.

Design
3. Determine who should convene and lead the effort.
4. Mobilize and engage the right people.
5. Define the region to match the place, problem, and people.
6. Get organized.

Take Action
7. Facilitate scientific and public learning.
8. Develop an action plan.
9. Move from vision to action.

Evaluate
10. Learn as you go and adapt as needed.

TEN GUIDING PRINCIPLES

These principles are general guidelines for any work that crosses boundaries or aims to bring people together across diverse interests. They are based on practical experience in regional collaboration, and also on the theories and practices behind various topical concerns, such as regional planning (Henton, Melville, and Parr 2006; Innes and Rongerude 2005; Meck 2002; Quick 2006); ecosystem management (Clark and Minta 1995; Harris et al. 2001; Keiter 1990; 1996); multiparty negotiation (Susskind and Hoben 2004; Susskind, McKearnan, and Thomas-Larmer 1999); watershed governance (Donahue 1987; Kenney 1994; Western States Water Council 1998); and bioregional philosophy (C. Foster 1997; Sale 2000).

PRINCIPLE 1: IDENTIFY THE COMPELLING ISSUE OR CATALYST ■

Most people are not accustomed to working across boundaries. They focus instead on the tasks immediately within their smaller sphere of influence. Anything beyond that is considered someone else's responsibility. Social and political arrangements further discourage people from working outside their individual silos. Given these challenges, regional collaboration becomes compelling when people recognize that they are more likely to achieve their interests by working together than by acting independently. Typically, this happens when people are faced with an immediate crisis or a threat to their quality of life. In some cases, people begin to collaborate proactively, before a crisis or threat appears, to take advantage of opportunities and benefits that arise from working across boundaries.

PRINCIPLE 2: DETERMINE IF THERE IS A CONSTITUENCY FOR CHANGE ■

Acknowledging the interdependence of interests is just a start. To launch a regional initiative, people must also want to change their situation for the better. Of course, it helps if people agree at least in broad terms on the general direction of that change and are willing to form working relationships among diverse interests. Such a constituency for change generates traction on the issue at hand among the broader public and the decision makers. It also helps to create momentum that can carry regional work over any initial inertia and through early obstacles. For these reasons, it is important to assess the level of interest in the issue at hand and determine whether people are ready to begin working together toward a better future.

PRINCIPLE 3: DETERMINE WHO SHOULD CONVENE AND LEAD THE EFFORT ■ Regional initiatives require a certain type of leadership. In contrast to exercising authority by taking unilateral action—a command-and-control model of leadership—regional leaders readily cross jurisdictions, sectors, disciplines, and cultures to forge alliances with people holding diverse interests and viewpoints. They invite people to take ownership of a shared vision and values, and they work hard to bridge differences and nourish networks of relationships. To move in the desired direction, regional leaders share power, mobilize people, synthesize ideas, and assemble resources. In the midst of this action, they provide integrity and credibility and advocate for the integrity of regional partnerships. They also show a high tolerance for complexity, uncertainty, and change; and they emphasize dialogue and relationship building by respecting the diversity of ideas and viewpoints. Respect builds trust, which in turn fosters communication, understanding, and eventually agreement. Recruit people with the above qualities wherever you may find them.

PRINCIPLE 4: MOBILIZE AND ENGAGE THE RIGHT PEOPLE ■ If the objective of regional collaboration is to advocate for a particular interest or outcome, the process requires a different group of people than if the aim is to resolve a multiparty dispute or to advance an agenda that includes multiple interests. In these latter cases, it is best to be as inclusive as possible by engaging people interested in and affected by the issue, those needed to implement any potential recommendation (that is, those with authority), and those who might undermine the process or the outcome if not included. Think carefully about the roles and responsibilities of existing jurisdictions and agencies, and keep in mind that there may be people outside the region who need or want to be involved. Also, keep an eye out for potential collaborative leaders.

PRINCIPLE 5: DEFINE THE REGION TO MATCH THE PLACE, PROBLEM, AND PEOPLE ■ The way in which people define a region naturally flows from their interests and concerns. Regions are most often defined in one of two ways—either rooted in a sense of place, or based on the "territory" of the problem. Natural ecological boundaries—such as watersheds, ecosystems, and wildlife habitats—can help inform the appropriate definition of a region, but in the final analysis the region must engage the hearts and minds of people and appeal to their shared interests. Recognizing the precise physical boundaries of a region is often less important than clarifying the core area of interest. Boundaries can be soft and flexible, adaptable to changing needs and interests. In sum, the region needs to be large enough to capture the problem, and small enough to get traction among people whose interests are at stake.

PRINCIPLE 6: GET ORGANIZED ■ Given that regional collaboration brings together people and groups from multiple jurisdictions, sectors, and disciplines, it is critical to be clear about how the conversation will be conducted. The more diverse and complex the conversation, the more it helps to articulate a common understanding of the goals, roles, and responsibilities of the participants. In short, the participants need to get organized (by clarifying operating protocols) and assemble the necessary resources (i.e., people, skills, information, and funds), preferably before they jump into dialogue on substantive issues.

Sometimes all of these resources and capacities must be developed from the ground up, but the more common experience is to borrow or leverage the resources and capacities of groups already working in the region. In fact, most regions have the necessary resources and the capacity to organize them. These resources simply need to be identified and better coordinated to be used more effectively.

PRINCIPLE 7: FACILITATE SCIENTIFIC AND PUBLIC LEARNING ■ Learning is a key part of working across boundaries. Participants confront new information and new ideas from every angle. They face mountains of scientific and technical data. People may be skeptical about information that comes from outside their jurisdiction or area of expertise. To complicate matters, existing information is often at the wrong spatial scale to be useful, or it is scattered in multiple databases, each in a different format. Under such circumstances, building understanding and agreement is difficult at best. The most effective regional initiatives respond to these challenges by fostering joint learning, gathering and interpreting information as a regional group, and through joint fact-finding and similar processes.

PRINCIPLE 8: DEVELOP AN ACTION PLAN ■ People facing a regional problem or issue usually want to roll up their sleeves and get right to work. But it's well worth taking a little time up front to articulate desired outcomes jointly and map out practical strategies to achieve those outcomes. Such an action plan is built around a shared vision for change. People negotiate among their desired outcomes until they have a package that everyone can agree on, and then they negotiate options for how to make those outcomes happen.

Every regional enterprise is unique, varying according to site-specific conditions, the nature of the issue, and the needs and interests of the people affected by the issue. Consequently, the most effective action plans are homegrown—developed by and for the people concerned about a particular region. Developing an action plan ensures that people are working toward a clearly stated and agreed-upon goal, and it spells out specific steps and tools for reaching that goal. A well-drafted action plan also allows people to assess their progress against the stated goals, adapt methods as needed, and document their success.

PRINCIPLE 9: MOVE FROM VISION TO ACTION ■ Once people agree on an action plan, the next step is to translate civic will into political will. Participants can start by understanding how the proposed regional action supplements other relevant efforts. Then they need to communicate their message to appropriate audiences, making it relevant and compelling. They need to demonstrate to political leaders and other decision makers that the political capital to be gained is greater than any political risk they may take in supporting the action. Outreach should rely on multiple strategies to inform, educate, and mobilize people (such as media, public events, publications, Web sites). Participants should also think carefully about linking their effort to established decision-making systems. Seek access to power—rather than power itself—by building bridges, coordinating actions, and doing things that would not otherwise get done.

PRINCIPLE 10: LEARN AS YOU GO AND ADAPT AS NEEDED ■ Taking action should be followed by evaluating what was accomplished. This civic learning process provides the political momentum to follow through on difficult problems. In some cases, there may be a need to sustain regional collaboration. Participants should begin by capturing, sharing, and celebrating their accomplishments, thereby reinforcing a sense of regional purpose and identity. Then it may be valuable to revise and renew the mission, adapting to new information, opportunities, and problems. Participants will also need to identify and develop the capacities to sustain the regional initiative—people (both current and new members), resources (money and information), and organizational structure.

CONCLUSION

These principles give practitioners a road map to work across boundaries, which can help clarify where you want to go (the goal or outcome), and how best to get there (strategies and steps to achieve that goal).

Given the unique needs and interests of different regions, the principles of working across boundaries should be adapted to each setting. This adaptation occurs in two ways (Brunner et al. 2005; Lee 1993; Scholz and Stiftel 2005). First, regional initiatives emerge to close a gap in governance. They create a new platform—a homegrown forum—to integrate previously independent systems of users, knowledge, authorities, and organized interests. Second, the political choices and policy decisions made by regional practitioners are adapted in response to experience on the ground as people learn by doing.

Taken as a whole, this set of principles informs the entire process of effective regional collaboration. It is well worth revisiting them frequently as a process unfolds. Although the actual strategies and tools used to work across boundaries will vary from one region to the next, these basic principles are universal—specific enough to help people navigate the challenges of working together on a regional scale yet broad enough to apply across a wide range of situations.

Keeping in mind that regional collaboration is more like political organizing than rational planning, figure 3.2 integrates the ten principles into four common stages of regional collaboration. These stages help clarify other key steps along the way of working across boundaries. Using a variety of illustrations and case examples, the following four chapters explain each stage of the process, emphasizing the relevant principles and practical strategies for effective regional collaboration.

Figure 3.2
Common Stages of Regional Collaboration

Diagnose	Design	Take Action	Evaluate
Determine the need for regional collaboration.	Match the process to the situation.	Formulate and implement actions.	Learn and adapt.
Identify the compelling issue or catalyst.	Determine who should convene and lead the effort.	Facilitate scientific and public learning.	Capture and communicate progress.
Determine if there is a constituency for change.	Mobilize and engage the right people.	Jointly name problems and frame options.	Evaluate process and outcomes.
Estimate the issue's geographic reach, complexity, and volatility.	Define the region.	Develop an action plan.	Determine if there is a need to continue.
Estimate the region's capacity to work across boundaries.	Get organized.	Move from vision to action.	Build a capacity to sustain.

███████ **Stage**   ███████ **Goal**   ☐☐☐☐☐☐ **Key steps**

Chapter 4

DIAGNOSE THE NEED FOR REGIONAL COLLABORATION

Before beginning any work across boundaries, those initiating the process should first diagnose the situation. Diving into such work without clearly understanding the problems or opportunities at hand is a recipe for frustration and probable failure. The basic diagnostic question at this stage focuses on principle 1: Why make the effort to work across boundaries? Another way to frame this question is: What is compelling people to consider regional collaboration? There must be a catalyst or a compelling reason for people to want to work together.

A compelling reason to collaborate across boundaries is not enough, however. For any such effort to get off the ground, the right group of people must want to work together in some constructive way (principle 2). In short, there must be a constituency for change. From the outset, it is important to clarify the scope of the issue that is driving people to work across boundaries and to assess their collective capacity to respond to the issue and to work together.

As illustrated in figure 3.2, four diagnostic steps determine whether a region needs to engage in regional collaboration, and if the region is ready to act. They must: (1) identify the compelling reason to act, as people in the region see it; (2) determine if there is a constituency for change; (3) estimate the geographic reach, complexity, and volatility of the issue; and (4) estimate the region's capacity to work across boundaries.

IDENTIFY THE COMPELLING ISSUE OR CATALYST

Working across boundaries is tough and unfamiliar, and many people are reluctant at first to think and act regionally. Social and institutional arrangements impose a tremendous inertia on civic and political will. Many local issues, from mill levies to land use decisions to political leadership, are embedded in systems of boundaries. It stands to reason, then, that effectively organizing and leading a regional effort require a significant catalyst—a compelling purpose or reason to try a new transboundary approach to resolving issues.

As a matter of principle, regional collaboration is compelling when people realize that they are more likely to achieve their interests by thinking and acting interdependently than by acting independently. This gets to the heart of transboundary issues—by definition they are issues that no single jurisdiction can resolve on its own. It may seem obvious, then, that transboundary issues require jurisdictions to work together.

But simply saying that is easy compared to getting people genuinely to recognize and accept the need to work across boundaries. Most people strongly prefer to focus on their existing, well-defined jobs within the confines of their jurisdictions. They already feel overworked and undersupported. Regional collaboration promises to add more work, more responsibilities, and more demands on already thin resources and staff time. These real concerns can be overcome with a compelling enough purpose and some assurances that the benefits of working across boundaries will outweigh the costs.

What creates a compelling purpose? What drives people to recognize their interdependence and reach across boundaries? Research and on-the-ground experience suggest that nearly all regional efforts originate in response to one of three driving forces: (1) an immediate crisis, (2) an emerging threat, or (3) a promising opportunity. Within these broad categories are a number of more specific motivators that should be taken into account, but they typically occur as subsets of the three broad driving forces. These motivators include:

■ self-interest;
■ the absence of an alternative to regional collaboration;
■ frustration with gridlock and inaction;
■ public pressure and/or political opportunity to get traction;
■ a shared vision, goal, or sense of place;
■ a desire to close the gap between current reality and the desired future; and
■ a sense of responsibility and commitment to a particular place.

AN IMMEDIATE CRISIS ■ Some of the most notable examples of regional collaboration emerged in response to a crisis. In Minneapolis and St. Paul, the Metropolitan Council (one of the first regional land use institutions in the United States) was formed in 1967 to address significant surface and groundwater pollution in suburban areas. The pollution violated federal clean water standards, and an inadequate response from local governments provided sufficient motivation for the state legislature to create the Met Council. Likewise, the Chesapeake Bay Commission (comprised of representatives from Maryland, Pennsylvania, and Virginia) was created in 1980 in response to the rapidly declining health and productivity of the nation's largest estuary. A similar crisis led to the ongoing effort to restore the Everglades ecosystem in southern Florida.

In each of these cases, the crisis reached a tipping point. Conditions were perceived as so dismal that people feared they were nearing a point of no return. When the resource at stake is as essential as water, such a crisis usually resonates with people, and they become a constituency for change. A less obvious resource issue, such as soil erosion or noxious weeds, may be harder to sell, although no less serious a crisis.

AN EMERGING THREAT ■ While a crisis can be a strong motivator for regional collaboration, many challenges facing regions fall short of being imminent dangers or disasters. A more typical driver for a regional effort is a perceived chronic threat to the quality of life in communities, watersheds, and regions. The effort to organize a regional conversation in the Pawcatuck Borderlands, a rural and relatively unspoiled area along the Connecticut and Rhode Island border, was motivated in large part by a commonly perceived threat to the quality of life in the area. Likewise, the Calgary Regional Partnership began work on a regional land use plan in response to the impacts from unprecedented growth around that city.

The Great Valley Center in Modesto, California, was catalyzed by a combination of threats facing the region. Carol Whiteside, former mayor of Modesto and later executive director of the center, recalled that "[t]here was no single crisis here; rather we were seeing the consequences of thousands of small decisions made by balkanized local governments. Each might be acting in ways that made sense to themselves, but the result was rapid transformation" (Porter and Wallis 2002, 12).

Facing either a crisis or a longer-term threat is usually a unifying force that brings people together against one common concern, despite their differing interests. A crisis may be more immediately compelling, while a threat generally allows more time to raise public awareness and rally the troops. Some threats are so slow moving and insidious, however, that people may resist acknowledging or responding to them until they become more serious.

A PROMISING OPPORTUNITY ■ Syndicated columnist and noted regional thinker Neal Peirce once observed, "the only thing more challenging than a crisis may be the lack of one" (Parr, personal communication 2005). The third driving force for regional collaboration, then, is the desire to capture or build on opportunities. This catalyst is more proactive—it asks people to work across boundaries before a problem arises. Unfortunately, it is also often perceived as the least compelling reason to collaborate.

The Crown of the Continent is a wilderness region centered on Glacier and Waterton Lakes national parks in the state of Montana and the Canadian provinces of Alberta and British Columbia. Land managers and local citizens alike recognize that they live, work, and play in a special landscape, and this realization—more than any specific threat—is galvanizing action to protect and preserve the ecosystem as well as the surrounding communities and economies. More than 20 federal, tribal, provincial, and state agencies participate in the Crown Managers Partnership, a voluntary partnership aimed at sustaining the ecological health of the region. In a similar effort, nonprofits, business leaders, recreation and tourism interests, and citizens collaborated on a Crown of the Continent geotourism MapGuide produced by the National Geographic Society.

Urban regions can also be proactive, as exemplified by the grassroots collaboration in the greater Orlando area of central Florida. In this case, citizens and civic leaders wanted to find common ground on issues such as light rail, improving public education, and making a bid for the 2012 Olympics. They saw an opportunity for their region to be more competitive in a global economy and at the same time enhance the quality of life for regional residents. This was more than enough motivation for people from the private and public sectors in seven counties to form an online regional development program called myregion. Today, this initiative continues to be guided by citizen and nongovernmental interests.

When organizing around an opportunity, many initiatives walk a fine line between raising awareness of looming problems and potential threats and highlighting the unique qualities and assets of a region. Also, they often laud the many benefits of collaboration itself: improved working relationships, economies of scale, reduced costs through resource sharing, and so on.

No matter how compelling a crisis, threat, or opportunity may be, such a catalyst alone is not enough to initiate a regional effort. In fact, identifying a compelling purpose or interest is just the first step.

DETERMINE IF THERE IS A CONSTITUENCY FOR CHANGE

The second diagnostic step is to determine whether there is a constituency for change. In short, is there a critical mass of people aware of a common crisis, threat, or opportunity, and ready to work together in response? This raises several more questions: Who is interested in or affected by the issue? What jurisdictions and decision makers are needed to implement any outcome? Who might undermine the process or outcome if not included?

Once you identify the range of potential actors or constituents, the next step is to clarify their needs and interests. Are their interests similar, different but compatible, or conflicting? The classic book on negotiation, *Getting to Yes: Negotiating Agreement Without Giving In,* explains how to clarify people's interests (Fisher and Ury 1981). Taking the time to understand those interests reveals whether they are interdependent and whether regional collaboration is the best option for achieving them. The greater the degree of interdependency and the fewer options people have, the greater the likelihood that regional collaboration is appropriate.

In the final analysis, it is important that all parties agree on the basic nature of the challenge even though they may disagree on why a particular issue is important and compelling. Also, people must believe that they are more likely to advance their interests through regional collaboration than by acting unilaterally.

ESTIMATE THE GEOGRAPHIC REACH, COMPLEXITY, AND VOLATILITY OF THE ISSUE

The next diagnostic step is to estimate the geographic reach, complexity, and volatility of the regional issue or opportunity. While a more rigorous definition of the region will emerge over time, it is important to clarify up front whether the issue can be framed in such a way that it captures the territory of the problem (or opportunity), resonates with people, and is workable. There is a tendency in many regional initiatives—particularly at the outset—to become so enamored with boundaries that one forgets what they represent.

"[P]roblem-solving is what regions are all about. They serve merely as the rationale for getting something done. . . . Boundaries are important, but for reasons that transcend those of the region itself. Human beings, for some innate reason, feel more comfortable functioning within defined parameters. It is intrinsically important for them to belong somewhere" (C. Foster 1990, 3). That said, people often spend too much time and energy hovering over maps trying to delineate a precise regional boundary. In reality, many well-functioning regions have multiple identities and fuzzy or shifting boundaries. Delineating the precise boundaries of a region is usually less important than clarifying the core area of interest and activity. Moreover, boundaries do not have to be exact and can even be fluid as the nature of the problem and people's interests change.

During this diagnostic step, the idea is to develop a preliminary sense of the territory of the problem and to clarify the complexity and volatility of the issue. How many jurisdictions might be involved? What is the history of relationships among potential participants? Do they have a track record of working together or not getting along? What do we know (or not know) about the scientific and technical aspects of the issue? These and similar questions can help diagnose the scale of the issue and the need for collaboration.

ESTIMATE THE REGION'S CAPACITY TO WORK ACROSS BOUNDARIES

The fourth and final key diagnostic step is to establish whether the region has the capacity to work across boundaries. The focus of this analysis is not on determining whether the region currently has the capacity to achieve its ultimate goals, but on whether it has sufficient resources to get the ball rolling and build the necessary capacities over time. A first step is to inventory the region's assets, particularly funding, organizational capacity (such as the ability to network, manage mailing lists and phone trees, and convene meetings), and basic information (e.g., maps). It is also important to ascertain how much people know about the issues and who is best able to influence other people.

Just as no single person or group is likely to have the power or authority to address a regional issue, no one will likely have all the necessary resources. The best way to assemble these resources is to identify what assets various partners are willing to share and bring to the effort, and what, if any, resources are missing.

This inventory should be weighed against a clear picture of the major barriers to regional collaboration and how they might be overcome. A related consideration is how external events, such as political factors and ecological imperatives, might affect the scope and timing of any regional effort. Finally, reflect on what can be learned by past attempts to address this issue. There may be pitfalls to avoid as well as opportunities to leverage.

SITUATION ASSESSMENT: ONE METHOD TO DETERMINE READINESS

In some cases, a region may be able to uncover answers to these diagnostic questions with existing knowledge and information. That is not always possible, however. Also, people considering launching a regional effort may want to crosscheck their understanding of the issues and drivers against a larger group of stakeholders. Doing so helps ensure the legitimacy, credibility, and transparency of any subsequent work.

One of the best ways to determine whether a region is ready to focus on regional collaboration is to conduct a situation assessment. This tool allows a potential convener—the person or organization interested in potentially hosting a regional forum—and all other stakeholders to begin developing a common understanding of the substantive issues, the diversity of viewpoints and interests, and alternatives to regional collaboration. It helps people understand the history and dynamics of a particular issue or situation and clarifies the incentives of the various parties to engage in regional collaboration.

A situation assessment can also be a vehicle to help people understand the costs and benefits of acting independently rather than regionally and cooperatively. Moreover, people learn about each other's interests and values through an impartial assessment process, and this helps build understanding, trust, and working relationships.

The process of conducting an assessment typically follows the steps outlined in figure 4.1. The information gathered during the assessment allows stakeholders, including the convener, to determine if the minimum conditions exist for regional collaboration and to begin designing an appropriate regional platform (Susskind, McKearnan, and Thomas-Larmer 1999). In short, a situation assessment can provide answers to the diagnostic tests presented above.

To initiate an assessment, a sponsor—typically a coalition of organizations when it comes to regional land use or water issues—decides that

Figure 4.1
How to Conduct a Situation Assessment

SPONSOR:*

Decide ➤
Is an assessment needed?

Retain a credible, impartial assessor.

Make a preliminary list of stakeholders to interview.

ASSESSOR:**

Initiate ➤ the assessment.	**Gather** ➤ information.	**Analyze** ➤ interview results.	**Design** ➤ a collaborative process (if appropriate).	**Share** the assessment with stakeholders.
Make a preliminary list of issues to explore.	Explore and write down stakeholders' key concerns and interests.	Summarize concerns and interests without attribution.	Identify stakeholder groups that would need to be involved.	Distribute a draft report and solicit comments from stakeholders.
Develop an interview protocol.	Assess stakeholders' willingness to come to the table.	Map areas of common and opposing interests.	Draft a suggested work plan for addressing key issues.	Ask interviewees to verify its accuracy and completeness.
Arrange confidential, face-to-face interviews with all relevant stakeholders.	Identify additional stakeholders to interview.	Identify opportunities for mutual gain.	Draft suggested ground rules for constructive communication.	Incorporate suggested changes and distribute a final draft.
	Continue interviewing until no new information arises.	Identify obstacles to reaching agreement.	Estimate the costs of supporting the process.	Help the sponsor and other stakeholders decide whether to proceed with a facilitated, collaborative problem-solving process.
		Assess the likelihood of reaching agreement.		

*A sponsor is any person or group interested in assessing a situation and the feasibility of a facilitated dialogue.

**An assessor must be impartial, a discerning listener, and experienced in building working relationships and agreements.

Source: Adapted from the Consensus Building Institute (1998).

an assessment would be useful and retains a credible impartial assessor. This person should be viewed by all stakeholders as nonpartisan and should have some understanding of the issues at stake and the institutional context of the issue. The assessor should be an effective interviewer and a discerning listener, since interviewing is the primary method of gathering information during the assessment. He or she should have a clear mandate from the sponsor, including an understanding that the assessor operates autonomously and will make recommendations based on his or her best judgment.

Working together, the sponsor and assessor make a preliminary list of stakeholders to interview, develop an interview protocol (using the diagnostic questions presented above when appropriate), and invite stakeholders to participate. The assessor typically reviews appropriate documents to learn more about the issues and parties, and then conducts interviews either one-on-one or in small groups of people with similar interests. Most assessors prefer to conduct interviews face-to-face, but sometimes telephone interviews are more practical.

Based on our experience, the framing of interview questions is very important. Discovering and clearly identifying the catalyst for regional collaboration may not be easy. Most people do not intuitively think regionally, and the term *region* itself may be an unfamiliar frame of reference. Asking, "What regional issues does your community face?" is rarely a good conversation starter. It's more apt to generate a blank stare.

A more effective question might be, "What is most important to you and your community?" Answers will vary as the question is asked across different sectors of the region, but common themes will emerge. People may name or describe various issues, some of which will be similar or related. They will also use different terms and vocabularies that reflect the nuances of their interests. It is important to capture both the shared themes and different perspectives (and terms of reference).

With a list of the most important issues in hand, participants can back into an analysis of whether these issues are truly regional in nature and thus may require some type of regional response. An appropriate line of questioning might go something like this.

- Does one or more of these issues cut across multiple jurisdictions, sectors, or disciplines?

- Does any single entity have the power or authority to address this issue?
- Is there an issue that can be addressed best (or only) through regional collaboration?

The answers to these questions begin to clarify whether there is a compelling reason to think and act regionally.

Once the interviews are complete, the assessor prepares a report that synthesizes the findings and conclusions along with one or more options on how the stakeholders might proceed. Depending on the scope of the issue and the number of people involved, the reporting format may be a conference call, a two-page memo, or a twenty-page analysis. The report is typically distributed to the people interviewed and to anyone else who might be interested in the issue. The objective of this reporting function is twofold: to validate that the assessor has accurately captured the needs, interests, and options as articulated by the interviewees; and to determine how, if at all, to move forward. The information gathered during the assessment allows stakeholders, including the sponsors, to tailor a process to match the situation. By engaging the right people and documenting their concerns and interests, an assessment is an important first step toward a credible, legitimate framing of the issues. It can also help the sponsor draft a compelling regional narrative (box 4.1).

A situation assessment does not always lead to full-blown regional collaboration. In some cases, the assessment will conclude that the region is not ready. People may disagree over the urgency and nature of the problems; decision makers may have other priorities. Citizens may be apathetic, or may not yet see the value in working with or learning from their neighbors throughout the region. In such cases, the situation may instead be ripe for simply raising awareness and beginning to build understanding of issues and interests.

CONCLUSION

Jumping headlong into working across boundaries without first diagnosing the situation would be like treating an epidemic without first identifying the disease. Rather than assuming that a compelling catalyst exists and the issues and people's interests are known quantities, it is always best to ask the people themselves—citizens, community leaders, business people, government officials, and elected officials. This can be done through informal

Box 4.1

Possible Outcomes of a Situation Assessment

Findings	• An inventory of the range of interests and likely participants
	• Clarification of values, interests, and concerns of all stakeholders (including decision makers)
	• Identification of areas of agreement and disagreement
	• A clearer understanding of how the public perceives the issues at hand
Options for Moving Forward	• Identification of legal, administrative, and practical (time and funding) constraints
	• Identification of opportunities and potential resources (funding, technical expertise, information, Web support, etc.)
	• A range of stakeholder-suggested solutions
	• Additional options identified by assessor
Recommendations	• An appropriate model or design for collaborative process
	• Suggested best practices
	• A forum to discuss findings, options, and recommendations
	• Next steps

surveys or through a more systematic situation assessment. Either way, it is crucial before moving forward to clarify the catalyst, identify a constituency for change, estimate the geographic scope of the issue, and inventory the region's capacity for working across boundaries.

Some people may argue that assessments are unnecessary, expensive, and time-consuming. In certain situations, where the key issues and stakeholders are well defined and agreed upon by all parties, an assessment may not add much value. Regional issues are rarely that easy to pigeonhole, however. More often such issues are defined by multiple parties, side issues, and jurisdictions; scientific and technical uncertainty; and a range of potential actions to address the problem—all of which create different views on what is important, relevant, and compelling. The risks of proceeding without an assessment are that key parties may be left out of the process (and may later undermine it), the right issues may not be addressed or framed appropriately, and the collaborative process may not be well suited to the situation.

A situation assessment is more than just a diagnostic tool to determine if a region is ready for regional collaboration. It also serves as a communication tool to help build a common understanding of regional issues, interests, and possibilities, as well as a design tool to help build the right regional platform given the unique needs and interests of a region.

Chapter 5

MATCH THE PROCESS TO THE SITUATION

A clear and accurate diagnosis of the situation allows participants to determine whether regional collaboration is an appropriate response to the problem or opportunity at hand. If people do in fact feel compelled to work across boundaries—if a constituency for change exists and people are ready to start working—then the time is ripe to decide how that work will proceed.

People are often tempted to roll up their sleeves and get right to work rather than first considering the options for how that work will be accomplished. But it is well worth taking time up front to design a thoughtful, efficient process for working across boundaries. A well-designed process is far more likely to draw people into the effort, help them stay focused on the region and the issues at hand, and achieve desired outcomes.

As presented in figure 3.2, there are four important steps in designing the right process for regional collaboration: (1) determine who should convene and lead the effort (principle 3); (2) mobilize and engage the right people (principle 4); (3) define the region (principle 5); and (4) get organized (principle 6). Some of this work started during the diagnostic stage. Now it is time to refine the constituency for change, the definition of the region, and the resources needed to work across boundaries.

DETERMINE WHO SHOULD CONVENE AND LEAD THE EFFORT

Once people agree that they have a compelling reason to work together, the next ingredient they tend to look for is leadership. Who is going to bring others together, organize the work, speak about the issue at hand, and be the voice for change? What sort of leader can work across boundaries and situations with a diverse range of interests?

People often think of leaders as having strong-willed, command-and-control, competitive personalities. The traditional sense of *leader* is just that—someone who holds the ultimate decision-making authority and is not afraid to exercise it unilaterally—that is, someone who wields power and tells other people what to do.

But working across boundaries requires a special type of leadership (Parr, Walesh, and Nguyen 2002). People who catalyze and coordinate successful regional efforts must possess characteristics that resonate across jurisdictions, sectors, disciplines, and cultures. Such collaborative leaders invite people to take ownership of a shared vision and values, and they work hard to bridge differences and nourish relationships. Collaborative leaders create legitimacy, credibility, and capacity by broadening participation, not hoarding power (box 5.1).

Box 5.1
Traditional Leadership vs. Collaborative Leadership

Traditional Leadership	Collaborative Leadership
Exercises unilateratal decision-making authority	Shares decision making
Communicates within a single network of like-minded people	Communicates among multiple networks of diverse interests
Works within a single jurisdiction	Works across multiple jurisdictions
Commits to an ideal or cause	Commits to a regional sense of place
Focuses on a limited number of issues	Focuses on a wide range of integrated but often competing issues
Seeks certainty and decisiveness	Accepts uncertainties and adapts as needed

To move in the desired direction, collaborative leaders share power and mobilize people, ideas, and resources. In the midst of this action, they provide legitimacy and credibility and advocate for the integrity of regional partnerships. They also show a high tolerance for complexity, uncertainty, and change. They emphasize dialogue and the building of relationships by respecting a diversity of ideas and viewpoints. Respect builds trust, which in turn fosters communication, understanding, and eventually agreement.

Collaborative leadership is also based on a special set of values—including inclusiveness, sharing of power and responsibilities, transparency, and commitment to partnering—that differ from the values of conventional leadership.

LEADERSHIP ROLES ■ As a regional initiative unfolds, different leaders may step forward at different times to fulfill different roles (figure 5.1). Rarely is one person or one group well suited to fill every leadership role that arises. At the start of a regional conversation, it is essential to have pioneers—entrepreneurial people who see problems or opportunities and/or have a regional vision and the ability to make it compelling to others. It is also important at the start to find one or more sponsors—a person

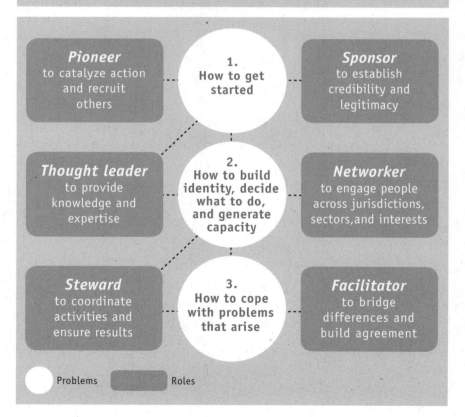

Figure 5.1
Leadership Roles for Regional Collaboration

Pioneer to catalyze action and recruit others	**1.** How to get started	**Sponsor** to establish credibility and legitimacy
Thought leader to provide knowledge and expertise	**2.** How to build identity, decide what to do, and generate capacity	**Networker** to engage people across jurisdictions, sectors, and interests
Steward to coordinate activities and ensure results	**3.** How to cope with problems that arise	**Facilitator** to bridge differences and build agreement

○ Problems   ▢ Roles

or group who can help create the credibility and legitimacy for a regional initiative.

Typically, although not always, those who sponsor or convene regional initiatives are in positions of leadership and hold a stake in the proposed regional action (Susskind, McKearnan, and Thomas-Larmer 1999). The sponsor can be from any sector, but must be a credible voice across sectors, jurisdictions, and disciplines. The role of the sponsor or convener is often self-selected; however, an individual or organization who is interested in a specific regional issue or outcome but who lacks the will or ability to convene an initiative can introduce the idea to those who are well positioned to launch a regional effort effectively.

As the regional conversation unfolds, a different kind of leader may be needed to build regional identity, decide what to do, and generate the capacity to act. Thought leaders provide knowledge and information, while networkers mobilize and engage other people across jurisdictions, sectors, and interests. When problems arise, it is important to have a facilitator to bridge differences and build agreement. Finally, every successful regional initiative needs a steward—someone to coordinate activities, provide follow-through on action items, and ensure results.

COLLABORATIVE LEADERSHIP IN ACTION: THE CASE OF CUMBERLAND REGION TOMORROW ■ Cumberland Region Tomorrow, based in Nashville, Tennessee, illustrates these various leadership roles and how they play out on the ground. In response to concerns about the region's growth and development patterns and their impact on the quality of life, the Vanderbilt University Institute for Public Policy Studies and *The Tennessean* daily newspaper sponsored a report on the region's assets and challenges, written by syndicated columnist Neal Peirce and urban policy expert Curtis Johnson (Peirce and Johnson 2000). In launching this effort, the institute and the newspaper served as pioneers. The report resonated with many of the region's citizens and stakeholders, prompting Vanderbilt University and the Greater Nashville Regional Council to sponsor a one-day regional planning summit. Local and national speakers shared insights and concerns about the current state of the region and presented best practices from other regions faced with similar growth issues.

While these sponsors were putting together the regional planning summit, they were also exploring whether the region would benefit from establishing a nonprofit entity similar to Bluegrass Tomorrow (Kentucky), Central Carolina Choices (North Carolina), or New Jersey Future. They gathered a diverse group of people as thought leaders and networkers to define the proposed organization's mission and goals, to begin raising funds, and to recruit a founding board of directors. Shortly thereafter, the board launched Cumberland Region Tomorrow as a private, nonprofit, citizen-based organization that works with the public, private, and nonprofit sectors.

The transition from thinking about some sort of regional initiative to establishing a regional platform through the organization of Cumberland Region Tomorrow required yet another kind of leadership. The organization has benefited from having a board of directors and two dynamic executive directors who have served as regional networkers and stewards. Importantly, the board cochairs also often serve as facilitators for conversations that would likely not happen without their credibility and evenhandedness.

These leadership characteristics have enabled Cumberland Region Tomorrow to form relationships and alliances with a wide range of the region's stakeholders, including local and regional chambers of commerce, city and county officials, the development community, business leaders, academic and civic leaders, natural resource managers, and environmental advocates.

Having provided the integrity and credibility necessary to organize and coordinate diverse regional stakeholders, Cumberland Region Tomorrow is now facilitating a strategic planning effort to prioritize and address critical regional issues. In so doing, the organization continues to provide leadership for the region by helping stakeholders transform their vision and hopes into practical, achievable action items. In this case, collaborative leaders emerged primarily from the private sector and the university community. In other situations, collaborative leaders emerge from elected officials (as in the Calgary Regional Partnership), public administrators (as in the Crown of the Continent Ecosystem Managers Partnership), or nongovernment organizations (as in the Regional Plan Association in New York, New Jersey, and Connecticut).

BUILDING LEADERSHIP CAPACITY ■ A number of regional initiatives place such a high value on collaborative leadership that they have created formal mechanisms to build a cadre of regional leaders with the desired values and aptitudes (Alliance for Regional Stewardship 2002). For example,

Leadership Middle Tennessee is an annual leadership institute serving the ten-county region around Nashville. Participants include community, business, and government leaders with a demonstrated commitment to community and regional issues. The curriculum for each year's eight-session class is designed to reflect current regional issues. Typically, participants hear keynote and informational speakers, observe demonstration projects, and go on field trips and site visits. Each participant also completes a project relevant to his or her professional work.

Similarly, the Sierra Leadership Institute, a program of the Sierra Business Council based in Truckee, California, is an annual week-long workshop aimed at improving civic leaders' skills in negotiating, communications, and collaborative problem solving. To date, more than two hundred people have graduated from the institute and now work throughout the Sierra region, collaborating on business, community, and environmental issues.

In both examples, participants cite such leadership institutes as important vehicles for networking with peers and as bridges to the directors and staff of their regional initiatives. In short, leadership institutes can encourage collaboration among independent partners throughout the region, while also building broad and deep support for the sponsoring regional initiative. Both of these outcomes are significant steps toward healthy, sustainable regional stewardship.

Collaborative leadership may strike some as an oxymoron, but the values and traits of such leadership increasingly are coming to the fore as more people engage in regional work. That is one of the strengths of regional collaboration—a variety of leadership roles are available, and many different people can fill them. A region's capacity for collaborative leadership stems in part from the participation of individual people, but also from the region's ability to nurture and support a culture of collaboration. Leadership seminars and institutes such as those described above are effective ways to do this. But it is equally important to infuse collaborative values into the daily work of meetings, phone calls, emails, and all the other myriad interactions that are at the heart of working across boundaries.

MOBILIZE AND ENGAGE THE RIGHT PEOPLE

Working across boundaries requires stepping outside of individual silos and peering over the fence into a neighbor's yard. For those unaccustomed to these broader horizons, the view might come as a surprise. Some of the yards are empty, their owners hidden indoors or away on travel. Other yards are full of people busy with gardening, lawn mowing, and taking out the garbage. Principle 4 asks, When it comes time to reach out to all these people, how will you do it? Who needs to be included? How do you reach people who are not in plain view? How do you know that you have found all the "right" people? And how do you mobilize and engage them to participate actively in the regional effort?

To be effective, regional initiatives must engage the right people and build a constituency for change. Chapter 4 introduced this type of constituency and how to determine whether such a group already exists in a region. It is not unusual, however, for a nascent regional initiative to help build such a constituency, either from some small beginning cluster of interested people or from scratch.

At this stage, being as inclusive as possible ensures that the initiative will be broadly supported by people with ownership in both the process and its outcomes. What does it mean to be inclusive? In broad terms, there are three categories of people who must be engaged for a process to be legitimate, credible, and effective. First are those people and groups who are interested in and directly affected by the issue; second are those needed to implement any potential recommendation (that is, those with authority); and third are those who might undermine the process or the outcome if not included.

This inclusive approach garners input and support from the widest possible group of stakeholders. Being inclusive creates a sense of buy-in and ownership from the start, empowering people to participate in identifying the issues or problems, framing solutions, and determining what actions to take. This also helps to minimize opposition late in the process because all the stakeholders have had a say in shaping the proposed actions.

In these respects, building a constituency for change is more like organizing a political campaign than engaging in a conventional planning process (McKinney and Essington 2006). A conventional planning process includes public scoping and input, but the decision makers themselves draft options, choose the preferred option, and finalize the plan. In contrast, building a constituency engages the stakeholders from the outset in naming and framing the problem and its possible solutions, and the stakeholders themselves (typically including the decision makers and officials responsible for implementation) design the proposed action. In this way, approval is built in from the beginning. When a diverse, broad-based constituency guides the process, it will more likely produce outcomes with which all participants can live.

Engaging the right people also means recruiting people with vision, passion, and commitment. Who are the champions or boosters in the region? They are likely to be civic leaders, but potential champions also may be government and elected officials, business owners, and ardent volunteers. They may be people who embody the values of collaborative leadership (box 5.1), or those who have the skills and aptitude to fill the different roles typical of most regional efforts (figure 5.1). Sometimes an organization can be a champion even when no one person within the group plays that role. Organizations provide a low-profile way for people to contribute actively while remaining anonymous, or at least sharing the limelight with a team.

In many regions, a nascent sense of regional identity and perhaps even a constituency for change already exist, although the constituency may be scattered and disorganized. To begin shaping a more cohesive constituency, avoid reinventing the wheel. Build on any existing social networks that already span sectors, institutions, and disciplines. Convene people to identify issues, share aspirations, and build relationships.

In some cases, a slightly different approach is more effective. When an opportunity (rather than a threat or crisis) is catalyzing regional action, it often makes sense first to build a coalition among people with similar interests, roles, or responsibilities before mobilizing and engaging other stakeholders. In the Yellowstone to Yukon Conservation Initiative (Y2Y) in the intermountain western states and Canada, for example, the core actors are conservation organizations, which then reach out to governments, businesses, and others interested in or affected by regional conservation issues. Similarly, the Calgary Regional Partnership is composed exclusively of local elected officials in 19 jurisdictions. These officials then engage other stakeholders on a project-by-project basis.

Coalitions need to be mindful of engaging the right people, again erring on the side of being more rather than less inclusive. It might be helpful to think in terms of a series of concentric circles and levels of representation (figure 5.2). The innermost circle is the core group or coalition (e.g., conservation groups in the Y2Y initiative, or elected officials in the Calgary partnership). In the next circle are other key stakeholders who might be

Figure 5.2
Levels of Representation

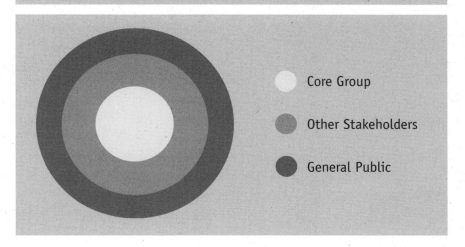

- Core Group
- Other Stakeholders
- General Public

needed to implement any recommendation or outcome and/or those who might undermine the process if not included. In this respect, it is critical to acknowledge the authority of existing institutions and decision makers and to engage them appropriately. Finally, the largest circle includes the general public. The challenge here is to inspire and engage residents of a particular place. It is also important to keep in mind that there may be people and organizations outside the region who need or want to be involved.

This coalition approach to representation allows the core group to build a sense of identity and purpose and to shape an initial course of action. The risk is that people not included in the core group—other stakeholders or the general public—may feel alienated if not included in the initial naming of problems and framing of solutions. Once alienated, it may be difficult to fully engage some people in a constructive way. This is particularly true in reference to existing jurisdictions and decision makers.

If the intent of a regional initiative is to shape or influence land use policy (or any public policy change requiring action by elected officials or government agencies), it is essential to link the effort to the appropriate formal decision-making process and/or institution (McKinney and Essington 2006). Government participation in such efforts is essential, but it need not drive the effort. Both top-down and bottom-up efforts can be successful, as long as they are strategically linked to the formal decision-making process.

The task of mobilizing and engaging the right people can be challenging. Two of the most common obstacles emerge when key parties choose not to engage and when civic and political wills are not aligned.

WHAT IF KEY PARTIES WILL NOT PLAY? ■ Imagine a fast-growing metropolitan region that includes 24 separate municipal jurisdictions. Over the years, the various jurisdictions have worked together under the umbrella of a regional association to share information and network, advocate for the region, provide research on regional issues, and provide a forum for stakeholders on regional issues. As growth and its consequences continue, most of the jurisdictions agree that it is time to create a regional growth management plan that integrates social, economic, and environmental values.

Unfortunately, the largest jurisdiction—the one with the most people, most money, and thus the most power—decides that it is not in its best interest to craft such a plan. It is concerned that the regional association has not been particularly effective over the years, questions the consensus-seeking, decision-making process of the association, and suspects that the proposed growth management plan is a veiled attempt by the surrounding jurisdictions to force it to share its tax revenues. How should the region proceed when one of the key jurisdictions refuses to participate or when other obstacles arise?

When key parties will not come to the table, there are several best practices that may be employed. The first and arguably most important strategy is to clarify why the jurisdiction has decided not to participate. Send a small delegation of other members of the regional association—members who have a good relationship with the right people in the largest jurisdiction—to clarify their interests and concerns and find out what would have to change to make them reconsider. It may be useful to revisit the decision-making and other operating protocols. It is often helpful at this point to distinguish among common interests, different but compatible interests, and conflicting interests.

Second, it may be a good time to pause and evaluate, and to celebrate progress to date. Rather than letting everyone focus on what has not and cannot be done, take some time to focus on what has been accomplished and how things might be improved. Chapter 7 provides additional guidance and tools to evaluate the progress of regional initiatives.

Third, go after low-hanging, nonthreatening fruit. In other words, focus on what you can do (based on common interests) without alienating any of the key parties. For example, the Crown of the Continent Ecosystem Managers Partnership has focused its energy on creating a regional database as a way to build relationships and a sense of common purpose. While some members of the partnership would like to be doing more policy development and advocacy for the region, they realize that they need to go slowly to get there.

Fourth, create a platform for affinity groups. Rather than take on a more ambitious agenda—such as a regional growth management plan—focus on a particular issue or topic that is of mutual or interdependent interest to most if not all of the members of the association. For example, the Metropolitan Council, the regional planning authority for Minneapolis and St. Paul, met with considerable fear and resistance when exploring how to integrate fast-growing communities outside the jurisdiction of the council into some type of coherent regional plan. Several of the participants agreed to create a working group to focus on open space and green infrastructure. The idea here is to identify specific projects that offer opportunities for mutual gain, rather than trying to take on too much too quickly and to get everyone to make a commitment to some larger agenda.

Fifth, and finally, it might be possible (though perhaps not always advisable or desirable) to resort to higher levels of authority. Perhaps there is a state, federal, or provincial government that has the legal or moral authority to compel all of the relevant jurisdictions to work together. This strategy is significantly different from the previous four practices in that it moves away from voluntary participation to mandatory participation. Given the likely consequences of such action, this strategy should be considered as a last resort.

WHAT IF CIVIC WILL AND POLITICAL WILL ARE NOT ALIGNED? ■

Sometimes citizens and their elected representatives have divergent views of the issues facing a region. They may disagree, for example, over how an issue is defined. Where one camp sees rampant growth diminishing a traditional way of life, the other camp sees economic opportunity and progress. They may also respond with varying degrees of urgency.

Residents of the San Luis Valley in south-central Colorado were concerned that their way of life and community character might be compromised by incremental growth and development. Some wanted the region's six counties and multiple towns to develop a common land use plan. A group of citizens representing a diversity of perspectives (including planning, conservation, real estate, newcomers, and watershed groups) called for convening a regional conversation in 2004. Unfortunately, the commissioners in the six counties, believing that they had the authority to manage land use individually—and collectively, if needed—were reluctant to convene or participate in any regional conversation. The federal land management agencies likewise believed that while regional collaboration may be a good idea, existing budget cycles and other priorities limited (or prohibited) their involvement. When people in positions of power and authority do not recognize the need for, or the value of, regional collaboration or refuse to catalyze and convene some type of regional conversation, what can and should be done?

This common problem works in the other direction as well. The September 11, 2001, tragedy sparked an exodus from New York City to the pastoral Neversink and upper Delaware River valleys spanning parts of New York, New Jersey, Pennsylvania, and Delaware. New homes and subdivisions quickly replaced family farms and woodlots, and strip malls and big-box stores soon followed. Growth rates soared to 40 percent a year, and school enrollments quadrupled within two years. The Delaware River Basin Commission and the National Park Service catalyzed and convened a regional discussion to prevent the degradation of water and recreation resources in the Delaware Water Gap National Recreation Area.

These two government agencies defined the region as the Tri-State Watershed (incorporating parts of New Jersey, Pennsylvania, and Delaware), and invited people from all walks of life to an exploratory meeting. During the discussions, it became clear that not all participants shared a common sense of how to define the region. They also differed on what issues to address and how to address them, suggesting that the government agencies had perhaps gone a bit too far in naming the issues and framing options and not being flexible in the face of different viewpoints.

The role and ability of government to convene effective collaborative processes are part of an ongoing debate in many professional circles. Some people argue that government cannot successfully organize and convene such efforts given its built-in institutional resistance and lack of responsiveness. Citizens, by contrast, often can provide more effective forums through organic, grassroots initiatives. Throughout the United States, a movement is growing where citizens, frustrated by government's lack of responsiveness, are convening place-based groups to address a variety of issues, ranging from growth management to endangered species to water allocation (Kemmis 2001).

Recent studies indicate, however, that participation by one or more levels of government is essential to the effectiveness of more ad hoc, citizen-driven processes (Kenney et al. 2000; Susskind, McKearnan, and Thomas-Larmer 1999; Susskind, van der Wansem, and Ciccarelli 2008). Governments not only provide financial and technical assistance, but also become critically important if the intent of a regional initiative is to shape or influence land use policy. Official government institutions, after all, constitute the formal public decision-making processes in our society.

Practical experience seems to suggest that neither the top-down nor the bottom-up approach is inherently superior, and in the final analysis the two ends of the spectrum need to come together to facilitate positive change. Whether a regional initiative is catalyzed and convened by citizens, nongovernmental organizations, businesses, or public officials, it can be most effective when the people initiating the process exercise collaborative leadership. In practice, it is people with competency and interest in a particular area who tend to step forward to catalyze and convene regional efforts.

Nevertheless, when there is a gap between civic will and political will, how should the civic entrepreneurs respond? What is the role of public officials and existing institutions in regional collaboration? Several best practices may be employed.

First, remember that regional collaboration is more about organizing a political campaign than rational planning per se. Therefore, it is often helpful to develop an explicit political strategy. Is it better to be bold and ambitious, or to take a more incremental approach and focus, at least initially, on a set of experiments or pilot projects? Keeping in mind that it is critical to build a constituency for change, is it better to be more or less inclusive, and how does the answer to this question change over time? When is the most important time to engage decision makers? If you spend too much time up front trying to get them on board, the process may get bogged down. If they are not on board from the beginning, it may be harder to implement outcomes.

Second, seek access to power, rather than power itself. In other words, move forward, keep decision makers informed, and continuously seek their input and advice. Do good work, but not so good that it overshadows or threatens the work of the political decision makers. Look for opportunities to transfer (or at least share) credit, and make it as easy as possible for decision makers to say yes.

Third, clarify the different roles of public officials and existing institutions, and determine what is needed most from them (Wondolleck and Ryan 1999). The most useful roles for decision makers are to initiate and convene meetings; provide opportunities for meaningful dialogue; provide logistical support; set a respectful, optimistic tone; help frame the issues for discussion; provide legitimacy and authority; and demonstrate a willingness to work together. Technical experts should be open minded; willing to listen, teach, and learn; and willing to contribute scientific and technical information. Stakeholders—including decision makers—should articulate their interests and priorities, including those of the broader public interest; explain the constraints within which they must operate (i.e., time, money, legal mandates, and information); ensure that any agreement is consistent with the laws and regulations; and ensure that any decisions can be defended and implemented within the agency.

Bringing people together from diverse interests and across a region is an ongoing assignment for any regional initiative. The work of building a constituency for change typically starts at the outset of any regional process, and the timing enables the stakeholders themselves to guide the process and take ownership of it. But this work must also carry on as long as the need for change continues to exist. Based on practical experience, public interest in the regional initiative will likely grow as the process moves closer to taking action on the ground. It is important to plan for this and prepare clear, concise talking points and background materials to bring newcomers up to speed and encourage their buy-in to the process.

As a regional constituency grows, new potential leaders may rise to the surface. In fact, the work of mobilizing and engaging people and that of organizing around collaborative leaders tend to overlap. Rather than thinking of these as separate steps in a linear process, treat them as twin threads running through the regional collaboration cycle, often occurring simultaneously and engaging many of the same people. Leaders may help trigger the process of mobilizing and engaging a constituency, and they will likely also arise from that constituency as it forms.

This work also overlaps with and braids into the process of defining the region and forming a shared sense of regional identity. Regions typically take shape around a geography of place or an identifiable "problemshed." Too often, the people themselves (and their interests) are left out of the geometry of drawing regional boundaries. The next step explores the critical link between place, problem, and people.

DEFINE THE REGION TO FIT THE PLACE, PROBLEM, AND PEOPLE

One of the challenges of working across boundaries is knowing which boundaries to cross and where to stop. Where, exactly, is the region that is ripe for collaboration, and what are its boundaries? Where does the region lay on the landscape, and where does one draw the most useful boundary?

When facing these questions, people typically focus on one of three ways to find an answer. Some people frame the region as a particular place, defined by geography. Others frame the region in terms of the scope of the problem they hope to address. The third way is less obvious and often overlooked: drawing a boundary around the people affected by and interested in the issue at hand.

People often spend a lot of time and energy drawing regional boundaries, hoping for some magic line that everyone will accept as the so-called correct one. It is ironic, then, that people are most likely to be overlooked when framing the region. Defining a region in terms of a problem or sense of place is so intuitive and self-apparent that people often fail to consider the interests of all the affected stakeholders and the scope of the region that would encompass those interests.

Stated this way, it becomes clear that the people who care about the problem or issue at hand should be a factor in how the region is defined. Without this critical piece, the puzzle of where to draw the boundaries will likely remain a sticking point throughout any collaborative process. In the case of the Pawcatuck Borderlands of Rhode Island and Connecticut, a key player, The Nature Conservancy (TNC), initially defined the region in terms of forest cover, its primary conservation interest. During subsequent conversations, other stakeholders argued that watersheds and commute-sheds were more appropriate benchmarks for defining the region.

Eventually, they all agreed that the boundaries vary depending on the specific issue and interests in question. This realization matches practical experience in other regions, strongly suggesting that the definition of the region must not only capture the geographic place and scope of the problem, but also must integrate people's interests. The region must fit the place, the problem, and the people.

PLACE-BASED IDENTITY ■ Some regions are naturally defined by geographic boundaries and place-based characteristics. Cape Cod, Massachusetts, for example, is identified first and foremost by its geography as a peninsula (figure 5.3). Other regions, such as the Crown of the Continent in the northern Rocky Mountains, are perhaps less geographically distinct, but hold together as unique regions because of their ecological integrity. Still other regions are defined by their edges. The Pawcatuck Borderlands is a region with a distinctive rural character that is threatened by growth and development along the adjacent I-95 corridor between Boston and New York City.

Place-based identity is perhaps most important if the intent of regional collaboration is to enhance or preserve the uniqueness of an area. The challenge in these situations is to help residents and visitors see and appreciate a region's unique and defining characteristics. As people learn more about the special qualities of the place where they live or visit, they can be more easily mobilized and engaged in activities to improve and sustain those characteristics.

One of the easiest and most common ways to build and reinforce a sense of regional identity is through maps. The Great Valley Center has generated a variety of maps to raise awareness and understanding of that region. One map features a satellite view of the region, a perspective from which the topographic boundaries of the vast area become obvious (figure 5.4). Mapping a community's or region's assets—a standard practice in most land use and natural resource planning—can also help define the region and foster regional identity. In its most basic form, mapping a region involves completing an inventory of the natural and built environment for a given place.

The National Geographic Society (NGS) is in the process of creating a series of *Geotourism MapGuides* that showcase a region's natural, cultural, and heritage assets. The maps are explicitly grounded in the concept of geotourism, which is tourism "designed to sustain or enhance the geographic character of a place—its environment, culture, aesthetics, heritage, and the well-being of its residents" (Center for Sustainable Destinations 2008). Geotourism mapping also can be used to mobilize and engage people from multiple jurisdictions and sectors to promote and sustain the qualities that most define the region.

Figure 5.3
Cape Cod and the Islands, Massachusetts

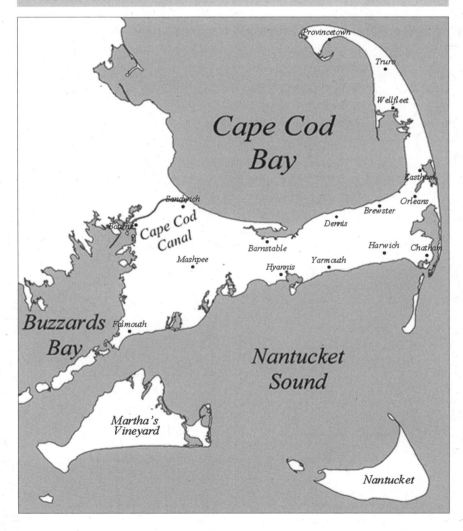

Figure 5.4
The Great Valley in Central California

Source: Central Valley Fund
(http://www.centralvalleyfund.com/process).

The *Geotourism Map-Guide to Appalachia* was the first such map to be completed, the result of a partnership between the Appalachia Regional Commission and NGS to help stimulate economic development in the region. The map includes more than 350 tourism destinations and events across the region, including artisan centers, scenic byways, traditional-music venues, outdoor recreation sites, festivals, and museums. Working with geotourism alliances in other regions, NGS has completed maps for Vermont, the Arizona/Sonoran Desert, and the Crown of the Continent and is currently working in Peru, Honduras, Guatemala, Romania, Norway, and Rhode Island. Each final geotourism map includes both a printed map and an online version.

PROBLEM-BASED IDENTITY ■ Regional initiatives also can be defined according to a particular problem and its problem-shed—the area that encompasses the problem and all the affected interests. Problem-sheds are often associated with particular functions or features, such as transportation corridors (Treasure Coast, Florida), watersheds (Columbia River Gorge, Oregon), wildlife habitat (San Bruno Mountain, California), dominant industrial base (Joint Venture: Silicon Valley Network, California), or growth and development patterns (Calgary Regional Partnership).

Regions come in as many shapes and sizes as the problems or issues they seek to encompass. For example, a regional effort to balance jobs and housing will likely span a commute-shed. A regional effort to enhance a metropolitan area's economy and quality of life through land use planning may focus primarily on the urban or built environment and give less attention to outlying rural areas.

The increasingly popular use of habitat conservation plans (HCPs) offers a good example of defining a region as a problem-shed. In rapidly growing states, particularly in the West and South, sprawling development patterns inevitably consume thousands of acres of natural wildlife habitat. The HCP mechanism grew out of a controversy over development plans that threatened several species of butterflies, including a federally listed endangered species, the mission blue, on San Bruno Mountain in the San Francisco Bay Area. A regional collaborative process clarified the butterflies' habitat needs (i.e., the problem-shed) and developed a conservation plan that allowed some development in designated areas, while setting aside nearly 90 percent of the butterfly habitat as permanent open space. The HCP also included a funding component, procedures for carefully monitoring development and minimizing its impact, and a long-term program of habitat restoration (Beatley 1995).

The positive experience of San Bruno led to a 1982 amendment to the Endangered Species Act (ESA) specifically allowing HCPs. Authorized under Section 10 of the ESA, HCPs allow for limited "take" of listed species in exchange for certain measures to protect and restore wildlife habitat. By 1999, the U.S. Fish and Wildlife Service had approved 290 HCPs, protecting 20 million acres, 200 listed species, and countless other species. As of March 2005, the nationwide number of HCPs had grown to more than 400 (U.S. FWS 2005). Not surprisingly, much of the deliberation in preparing an HCP focuses on the habitat needs and boundaries of the wildlife species in question. Given this problem-shed orientation, HCPs vary in their geographic scope. The region may be defined as a single parcel or property or as a large area involving many landowners, multiple governmental jurisdictions, and, in some cases, more than one species of concern.

PEOPLE-BASED IDENTITY ■ The people who live in a particular region may, over generations, develop a special sense of cultural identity that is distinct from neighboring regions and based in part on shared values. In the United States we recognize social value distinctions among the regions of New England, the Deep South, the Bible Belt, the Rust Belt, and southern California, for example.

The same sort of values distinctions also apply on a smaller scale, such as in the central Florida region around Orlando. When civic leaders there saw opportunities to manage the area's growth, transportation, and natural resources at a regional scale, they first surveyed residents to find out what their interests and values were, in part to determine whether this imagined region truly existed as a cohesive unit. They learned that the majority of respondents shared common concerns about the region's water supply, environmental health, economic prosperity, and education. No single problem or threat was pressing on the region, which could not readily be defined by the lay of the land. What united this region was its people and their shared values. The organization that arose to guide regional collaboration emphasized the central role of local residents by establishing an online resource called myregion.org.

Even in regions with more diverse values, regional collaboration often sparks greater awareness of the similarities among people and their interests, reinforcing a sense of regional identity. It is not unusual, for example, for rural and urban residents within a region to think initially that they have little in common with each other. Working together often brings to light shared concerns over issues such as water quality and supply, growth and open space, transportation, and fire management.

A REGION'S REGIONS ■ A single region may actually contain multiple regions, each with a different geography and meaning (K. Foster 2001). Most regions are likely to contain several of the following types of regions:

■ ecological regions based on the goods and services provided by large landscapes, such as air quality, water supply, water quality, and so on (e.g., Florida Everglades);

■ hydrological regions such as watersheds and river basins (e.g., Missouri River Basin);

■ metropolitan regions based on an urbanized footprint (e.g., Minneapolis–St. Paul metropolitan area);

■ megapolitan regions based on connected networks of metropolitan areas (e.g., New York City/New Jersey/Connecticut region);

■ megaregions or networks of metropolitan areas, connected by travel patterns, economic links, shared natural resources, and social and historical commonalities (e.g., the Great Lakes megaregion);

- economic regions based on trade flows, labor markets, and buying patterns (e.g., Great Valley, California);
- administrative regions based on legal and institutional boundaries (e.g., congressional districts, national forests and parks, counties, and municipalities);
- service regions based on service delivery territories (e.g., Metropolitan Water District of Southern California); and
- cultural regions based on language, arts, literature, and social norms (e.g., Pacific Northwest).

Another way to illustrate this idea of a region's regions is to look at the emerging megaregions of the United States (figure 5.5). All of them—no matter how large the metropolitan footprint—also include and rely on significant natural areas (bioregions). Cascadia encompasses not just Seattle and Portland, but the open space, habitats, recreational opportunities, and natural resources of the North Cascades, Puget Sound, the Olympic Peninsula, and the Pacific Coast. The Florida megaregion grows around the Everglades and includes coastline, islands, and the ocean itself. Even the established

Figure 5.5
Megaregions of the United States

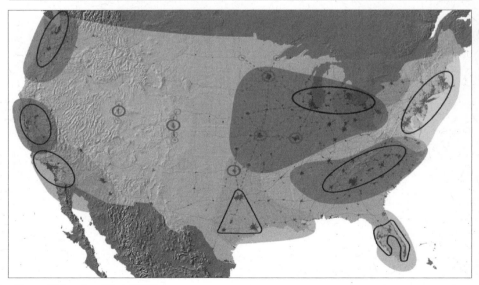

Source: Carbonell and Yaro (2005).

megalopolis of the Northeast cannot extricate itself from its codependency with coastal fisheries, the Adirondacks, Catskills, Delaware Water Gap, New York–New Jersey Highlands, Pawcatuck Borderlands, and other special places.

Clearly, these megaregions are defined not just by their urban centers, but by their natural ecosystems and resources as well. In every case, the natural areas provide resources the cities cannot live without—clean, copious water; food; open space and recreational opportunities; wood products; minerals; and energy. These natural amenities draw people to these regions. Ultimately, the cities and populations there will exist and grow only as long as their natural systems continue to support them.

The idea of a region's regions is consistent with some of the observations of the 1935 National Resources Committee, which concluded that it was futile to try to discern or define a single best kind of region. Rather, the early regionalists argued in favor of an adaptive approach where form follows function (C. Foster and Meyer 2000). A survey completed in 1998 found that regionalists continue to agree that there is no one, true region. Rather, different types of regions need not be mutually exclusive. "Watersheds, for example, can serve as 'regions of the mind' as well as 'problem-sheds'" (C. Foster and Meyer 2000, 20). These findings suggest that, at any given time, there is likely to be a particularly compelling issue that determines what region a group may focus on and what regional strategy might be appropriate.

METHODS OF DEFINING THE REGION ■ Regardless of the basis used to define a region—place-based, problem-based, people-based, or some combination—setting the most appropriate geographic boundaries for regional collaboration is rarely easy. The challenge can be magnified when working across cultural and international boundaries. Drawing a broad-brush outline (rather than strict, narrow lines) around the region makes it easier to include areas and interests as needed.

One of the most fascinating contributions of the 1935 study on *Regional Factors in National Planning and Development* is a method of defining a region in a way that captures both the territory of the problem *and* the people's interests (C. Foster and Meyer 2000). The report's nine characteristics of a region are as useful today as they were nearly eight decades ago (C. Foster and Meyer 2000).

1. Its territory should be as contiguous and compact—rather than fragmented—in outline as possible.

2. It should possess the maximum degree of homogeneity; i.e., it should exhibit marked homogeneity of elements and characteristics in its central core, and become progressively diluted toward the periphery. The boundaries themselves are in most instances transition zones rather than sharp lines.

3. It should possess unity, organic interrelationship, and cohesion; i.e., it should have unity in environmental characteristics to such an extent that it is or tends to be overlaid by a dominant type of cultural pattern embodying the works of humankind.

4. It should include all territory containing a major combination of resources; i.e., it should be an economic-natural unit in general terms.

5. It should include whole problem areas and not partial areas.

6. As nearly as possible it should include a total areal pattern of culture and works, and should not cut across such patterns.

7. It should be so delineated as to conform to existing regional consciousness and sentiments.

8. It should possess regional identity and such a uniqueness that a real consciousness will be quite compelling.

9. It should be of fairly large size; i.e., the largest area within which there is marked unity in physical and cultural elements.

This list of characteristics helps demonstrate the core principle at work here: the definition of the region must not only capture the place and the problem-shed, but also must integrate people's interests. The region must fit both the interests and the problem. The following questions can help in determining whether a region has the above characteristics.

With respect to place:
- Does the region resonate with the way in which most people define the social, economic, administrative, physical, and natural characteristics of the community or place?

- Is the region large enough spatially to capture the problem, but small enough to get traction politically?

With respect to the problem:
- Does the region adequately capture the problem area?
- Does it reflect natural boundaries, such as watersheds, transportation corridors, and wildlife habitat?

With respect to the people:
- Does the region reflect people's needs and interests?
- Will it inspire, mobilize, and engage people?
- Can you build on constituencies that are already present and bound your region in terms they can readily understand and support?
- Can you work through or with established organizations, rather than create wholly new regional efforts?

There are several ways to gather information to answer these questions, including interviews, surveys and polls, focus groups, maps and other visual methods, direct observation, and social maps. In the final analysis, it is worth keeping in mind the pragmatic advice of Charles H. W. Foster, a seasoned regional practitioner and scholar: "Regions have utility, not truth. They are a means to an end" (personal communication 2005).

GET ORGANIZED

Given that regional collaboration brings together people and groups from multiple jurisdictions, sectors, and disciplines, it is critical to be clear about how the conversation will be conducted. The more diverse and complex the conversation is, the more it helps to articulate a common understanding of the goals, roles, and responsibilities of the participants. In short, principle 6 states that the participants need to get organized by clarifying operating protocols and a communications strategy and assembling the necessary resources (i.e., people, skills, information, and funds), preferably before they jump into dialogue on the substantive issues.

Being deliberate at this stage can prevent many problems from cropping up later. Getting organized ensures that the participants will have clear and common expectations about the purpose of the forum and their roles and responsibilities. It provides rules of the road. At this point in a regional conversation, it is important to go slow to go fast. Most people will want to start discussing the substantive issues almost immediately. However, if they do not agree on the structure of their conversation, they may get muddled in procedural disputes in the midst of doing substantive work.

By documenting roles and responsibilities at the outset, getting organized provides a baseline against which progress can be measured. It also facilitates communication and clarifies which resources are needed to work across boundaries. In the context of regional collaboration, organizational strategies may take various forms, including a work plan and set of ground rules, memorandum of understanding (or terms of agreement), or business plan. Consider the following examples.

- The Calgary Regional Partnership's business plan articulates a set of overarching goals and then provides a detailed summary of each of the partnership's projects, including budget and staff requirements, strategies, and time lines for implementation.
- The Crown Managers Partnership is organized around a memorandum of understanding that clarifies the goals, participants, activities, and commitments to sharing resources.

Regardless of the name, an organizational strategy is most often developed by the participants during the process of assessing the situation; it is then revised and adopted during the first few meetings.

CLARIFY OPERATING PROTOCOLS ■ Operating protocols ensure that the participants have clear and common expectations about the purpose of a regional initiative and the roles and responsibilities of the participants. It is best for the participants to develop the operating protocols themselves, perhaps with the help of a facilitator. Typically, the protocols are revised and refined the first few times people meet. The process of developing such protocols helps participants learn to work with and trust one another and also allows them to develop some understanding of each other's needs and interests.

The basic issues and questions that should be addressed in operating protocols for a regional platform are described by Susskind and Cruikshank (2006).

- Identify participants and the constituencies they represent.
- Specify participants' responsibilities to each other and to their constituents.

- Clarify ground rules to govern behavior.
- Agree on how decisions will be made.
- Clarify the tasks of a regional facilitator.
- Agree on organizational management:
  - How will agendas be created, meetings recorded, and documents distributed?
  - How will the initiative engage in mutual learning and joint fact finding?

PREPARE A COMMUNICATIONS STRATEGY ■ Whenever two or more people work together toward a common goal, they must communicate. In informal situations, we do not think much about how that communication happens or precisely what form it takes. But in any serious effort to work on a regional scale, with all the attendant complexities of multiple players, diverse interests, jurisdictional boundaries, and intertwined issues, effective communication rises to the fore as a critical component for success.

Thoughtful, strategic communication allows us to: (1) identify the compelling issue(s) that will galvanize people to work across boundaries; (2) raise public awareness and interest; (3) build a constituency for change; (4) keep partners and constituents informed; (5) build political support; (6) organize and coordinate efforts among diverse interests; and (7) link outcomes to formal decision-making processes. In short, communication is how every aspect of regional work gets done, following a series of basic steps.

- Determine purpose: decide why you want to communicate—what do you hope to achieve?
- Identify audience: with whom do you want to communicate?
- Do a reality check: consider time, budget, staffing, other resources, and political constraints.
- Choose the right tools: match communication tools to specific purposes and audiences.
- Learn and adapt: seek feedback, and refine and adapt your communications as needed.

These same ingredients apply to any communications strategy, but they become even more crucial for success when working across a region that spans boundaries among jurisdictions, interests, areas of knowledge, culture, even language. To be able to work and foster cooperation across these boundaries, it is important to find a common vocabulary. Basic concepts often demand the most care in choosing that vocabulary. In the Crown of the Continent, for example, people rallied around *regional stewardship* but not *regional conservation*. Similarly, they embraced the notion of *networking*, while *collaboration* sounded too formal and coercive. In short, how the message is framed can be as important as the message itself if you want to reach your intended audience.

Focusing on communications also helps to spotlight logistical barriers that crop up when working across boundaries. Some government agencies, for instance, maintain firewalls and spam blockers that effectively stop any emails with more than one address in the "To" field. There may also be protocols prohibiting the sharing of phone numbers, street addresses, and other contact information. Crossing international boundaries for meetings and conferences often requires travel requests to be filed and approved weeks or months in advance, and travelers must obtain passports or visas. Such barriers exist at nearly every portal to transboundary communication—it is the nature of boundaries. Consciously thinking about how you will address these barriers can prevent or at least reduce difficulties.

ASSEMBLE THE NECESSARY RESOURCES ■ As discussed in chapter 2, many (if not most) regional efforts start out as informal networks or partnerships before evolving into more formal organizations. Nevertheless, even informal networks and partnerships need resources—people, skills, information, and funds to name just a few. Participants in the Lincoln Institute of Land Policy's 2001 policy dialogue on ad hoc regionalism observed that, while some regional efforts are embedded in well-established organizations, the more common experience is to borrow or leverage the resources of existing organizations to build a collective regional capacity (Porter and Wallis 2002). The following questions can help assemble the necessary resources.

- What resources—people, skills, information, funds—are needed and available to work across boundaries?
- Where can additional resources be found?
- Who can help identify sources of funds and assistance?
- How can available resources be used to stimulate more interest in the project?

While some regional efforts are supported by borrowing, mixing, and leveraging resources from participating individuals and organizations, others rely on grants from foundations and governments. One strategic question faced by any potential donor is whether it is more effective to invest in existing institutions, which may treat regional collaboration as simply one more thing to do, or to invest in creating new networks, partnerships, and organizations.

CONCLUSION

Designing a regional collaboration process should be a conscious, deliberate activity that is not left to chance. It is also best undertaken by the participants themselves, convened and organized by people who are willing and able to lead such an effort. Although these ideas may seem obvious, being explicit about the choices made during the design phase helps to ensure that the process remains open, transparent, and equitable.

Taking stock at the outset of any regional effort of what capacities and resources will be needed allows people to identify what assets they may already have and to acknowledge which resources and skill sets are lacking. Although this step is easily and too often skipped, it need not be arduous.

Regardless of the form taken by the final design and organizational strategy, capture these details in writing. They will become an important baseline upon which to look back, a record of promises made, and an accounting of which ideas worked and which were less fruitful. In the whirlwind of working across boundaries, nailing down such information is the best way to keep track of where you have been and to see a clear way forward.

Chapter 6

FORMULATE AND IMPLEMENT ACTIONS

D iagnosing and designing a regional collaboration process are the first two stages before taking action—addressing the issue at hand. This third stage should continue to emphasize the same qualities of earlier stages, that is, taking action should be deliberative, inclusive, and transparent. It should be planned and strategic, rather than merely reactive.

In most regional work, action occurs in several forms. It sometimes includes formulating changes in public policies to help and encourage people, agencies, and other groups to work across boundaries. Action also takes the form of participants jointly gathering and understanding scientific, legal, and other types of information. Such information becomes the basis for action planning and, ultimately, implementation of on-the-ground improvements that resolve problems.

FACILITATE SCIENTIFIC AND PUBLIC LEARNING

Nearly all efforts to work across boundaries face two distinct challenges with respect to learning. First, while citizens, policy makers, and scientists agree that land use, natural resource, and environmental policy should be based on the best available science (White House Conference on Cooperative Conservation 2005), producing scientifically credible information across multiple jurisdictions, sectors, and disciplines is often a challenge. Second, the scientific and technical information necessary to guide regional decisions must be perceived as legitimate and relevant in the eyes of all stakeholders in order to create a common foundation for understanding the issues in question. In sum, effective regional collaboration must facilitate both scientific and public learning.

Among the most promising strategies to facilitate the type of learning required for regional collaboration are those known as joint fact finding and collaborative learning (Adler and Birkhoff n.d.; Bingham 2003; Daniels and Walker 2001; Ehrmann and Stinson 1999; Karl, Susskind, and Wallace 2007; Susskind 1994). These strategies allow stakeholders and decision makers to work side by side with experts to seek agreement on what they know, what they don't know, and what they need to know in order to make timely, informed decisions (figure 6.1).

The central point in principle 7 is that when people learn together as a group, they are more likely to trust the information and give credence to one another's understanding of the issues. This builds trust and improves working relationships among diverse interests. It also creates a sense of ownership over the information and knowledge that the group needs to make good decisions, allows indigenous or local knowledge to be integrated with "expert" knowledge (Adler and Birkhoff n.d.), leads to more creative decisions, and clarifies the uncertainty commonly associated with regional land use, natural resource, and environmental issues. For these reasons, it is best to plan for and incorporate joint fact finding and collaborative learning into the process from the outset.

TOOLS TO FACILITATE LEARNING ■ During the past few years, several regions have used innovative computer technologies and workshop techniques to increase public participation, foster regional identity, create regional visions, assess the impact of alternative regional scenarios, and secure community support to implement regional goals and aspirations (Snyder 2006). These so-called decision support tools embrace the philosophy of joint fact finding and are designed to facilitate both scientific and public learning. We thus refer to them as "learning support" tools.

The menu of available tools may be organized and presented in several ways. PlaceMatters, a nonprofit organization dedicated to developing and applying learning support tools to land use, natural resource, and environmental issues, maintains a Web site that provides practitioners access to a growing list of case studies and a database of tools (PlaceMatters 2008). The Lincoln Institute of Land Policy has recently published several books that examine the application of learning support tools, albeit not necessarily in the context of regional collaboration (Brail 2008; Campoli and MacLean 2007; Hopkins and Zapata 2007; Kwartler and Longo 2008). Learning support tools may be used at any stage of regional collaboration and typically use some form of mapping and spatial information technologies,

Figure 6.1
Joint Fact Finding (JFF): Key Steps in the Process

PREPARE for JFF STEP 1	SCOPE of the JFF process STEP 2	DEFINE the most appropriate methods of analysis STEP 3	CONDUCT the study STEP 4	EVALUATE the study STEP 5	COMMUNICATE the results of JFF process STEP 6
Understand how JFF fits into consensus-building process.	Work with stakeholders to draft roles and responsibilities.	Translate general questions into researchable questions.	Undertake the work, checking back with constituents.	Use sensitivity analysis to examine the overall significance of scientific assumptions and findings.	Jointly present findings to stakeholders.
Document the interests of all relevant stakeholders.	Generate technical questions.	Identify relevant methods of data gathering/analysis, and highlight the benefits/disadvantages of each.	Draw on expertise and knowledge of stakeholders.	Compare findings to the published literature.	Scientists communicate JFF results to various constituencies and policy makers.
Work with a professional "neutral."	Identify existing information and knowledge gaps.	Determine costs and benefits of additional information gathering.	Review drafts of the final JFF reports.	Translate findings into possible policy responses.	Determine if further JFF is necessary.
Convene a JFF process.	Advise on methods for dealing with conflicting data and interpretations of facts and forecasts.	Determine whether proposed studies will enable stakeholders to meet interests.		Clarify remaining uncertainties and appropriate contingent responses.	
				Determine whether and how JFF results have (or have not) answered key question.	

Source: Susskind et al. (2007, 181–203).

such as a geographic information system. Mapping in this context refers to any methods used to elicit and record spatial data and thereby to facilitate scientific and public learning. Tools range from hand-drawn sketches to color-coordinated group drawings to 3-D computer models.

Learning support tools improve a region's capacity for scientific and public learning by engaging a diversity of citizens, stakeholders, and officials to identify problems; inventory conditions; analyze trends; generate and prioritize options; assess impacts; build consensus; implement effective solutions that cut across traditional borders of discipline, knowledge, sector, and geography; and monitor and update policies and plans. Across the board, these tools make complex information available to a wider audience because they summarize a large amount of information and present it in a visually accessible and engaging format. In this sense, learning support tools can be effective means of communicating expert and often diffuse knowledge in a manner that can inform public action (Norgaard and Baer 2005).

Figure 6.2 provides one simple way to visualize the range of learning support tools available. The overlapping circles represent four common needs or steps in regional collaboration, and the areas where the circles overlap suggest that some learning support tools can be used for more than one purpose.

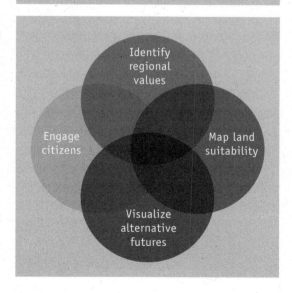

Figure 6.2
Common Uses of Learning Support Tools

Identify regional values

Engage citizens

Map land suitability

Visualize alternative futures

CHOOSING THE RIGHT TOOL ■ While learning support tools can serve as a useful aid in regional collaboration, if not well suited for a region's needs they can also present additional problems. As a first step, regional practitioners should identify exactly what they are trying to address and whether using a mapping or spatial analysis tool would help or hinder that effort. Box 6.1 summarizes some of the

Box 6.1
Benefits and Drawbacks of Learning Support Tools

Tools can help . . .	But tools may also . . .
serve as a catalyst for regional collaboration.	increase financial costs and time commitments.
increase transparency of decision making.	require specialized software.
promote adaptive management.	
facilitate broad participation.	exacerbate tensions among stakeholders if tools misrepresent their interests or concerns.
create various "what if . . . ?" scenarios.	
synthesize vast amounts of complex information into graphic representations.	require long-term contracts and maintenance agreements.

Source: Adapted from Quinn (2006).

benefits and drawbacks of using such tools to address regional problems. For example, understanding a region's needs and the types of tools available can help ensure that the tool a region uses maximizes its benefits while minimizing the costs.

As explained earlier, learning support tools can be used at various stages of regional collaboration, from the initial stages to evaluating and adapting regional efforts. While their use is not tied to a specific stage of development within a regional effort, tools should be selected deliberately to provide the kind of information people need to improve their understanding of the issues and their ability to construct a well-reasoned strategy for addressing those issues. Regions should also take into account the quality of available data as well as the assumptions that underlie each specific method (U.S. EPA 2000).

Choosing the right learning support tool can be difficult, given the wide variety of products and the limited amount of information available to help regions select the appropriate tool or model for their needs. Box 6.2 provides some practical guidance on selecting the most appropriate learning support tool in any given situation.

Box 6.2
Considerations in Selecting Learning Support Tools

Relevancy	Does the model provide pertinent information that meets the analytical needs of the region?
Resources	Are the model, computer requirements (hardware, software), and staff (number of people and their time) needed to support the system within the region's budget and infrastructure?
Model Support	Do the model developers, or does the model itself, provide sufficient support to understand and implement the model (e.g., model documentation, user discussion groups, training)?
Technical Expertise	Does the region have the technical expertise required to use, calibrate, and interpret the results of the model?
Data Requirements	Does the region have, or can it obtain, the data necessary to run the model?
Accuracy	Are the projections generated by the model reliable to a degree that is useful to the region?
Resolution	What amount of land and what level of detail can be modeled in a single scenario?
Temporal Capabilities	Can the model project outcomes for multiple time periods?
Versatility	Can the model project outcomes for multiple variables (i.e., land use, transportation, employment, housing, and environment)?
Linkage Potential	Can the model be linked to other models currently in use by or of interest to the region?
Public Accessibility	Can the model be run in an interactive public forum and display the results in a manner that is comprehensible to the general public?
Transferability	Can the model be applied to locations other than the one(s) for which it was developed?
Real-World Use	How extensively has this model been used in real-world situations?
Friendliness	Do you like how the system works?
Open Architecture	Does it provide flexibility to adapt to your needs?

JOINTLY NAME PROBLEMS AND FRAME OPTIONS

Once a region has achieved a sufficient level of scientific and public learning about the transboundary issues in question, it is time to name problems and frame options. More times than not, the action plan in most regional initiatives is implicit. The process of formulating an acceptable and effective strategy, however, is first and foremost a process of political engagement and thus should be as explicit and intentional as possible.

Regional collaboration requires a different form of politics than business as usual. Public problems—including regional land use, natural resource, and environmental issues—are most often framed by and for politicians, public administrators, and technical experts. Rarely do citizens, stakeholders, business leaders, or others have an opportunity to name problems, frame options, and consider the implications of alternative choices. Consequently, these people may feel disconnected from—if not also disillusioned by—the terminology and frameworks typically used to characterize such problems.

Recent research on public dispute resolution and deliberative dialogue, combined with the experience of regional practitioners, suggests that there are some common political practices required to work across boundaries (Mathews 2005). These practices allow all stakeholders to name issues and frame solutions for public problems jointly, which helps to foster ownership and commitment in the process and outcomes. Since no single institution or entity is responsible for or has the authority to address a multijurisdictional problem, the issues and potential solutions must reflect the interests and viewpoints of people who have a stake in the issue, those who are needed to implement any potential outcome, and those who might feel compelled to challenge the process or its outcome.

STEP 1: NAMING PUBLIC PROBLEMS ■ When people talk about their values, interests, and concerns, they are naming their problems. This is a political practice because the name we give to a problem guides the process of solving it. Who gets to participate in naming the issue, and the actual words used to name it, in turn shape who will likely engage in subsequent conversations, what options they will consider, and the range of choices and solutions that will emerge. Too often, issues are named by politicians, special interests, experts, or the media in ways that divide rather than unite an interested public. The best way to ensure that the naming of an issue resonates with people who are interested in or affected by the issue is to engage those people in naming it. The following questions can help name an issue.

- How does this issue affect you personally?
- What are the different ways of seeing this issue?
- How does this issue affect others?

STEP 2: FRAMING OPTIONS ■ Once a regional problem has been named, people will naturally want to talk about what can be done to solve it. During this step, participants propose options that become part of the framework for addressing the problem. This framing structures the future course of the conversation and any action that may emerge from regional collaboration. Just as with naming, how an issue is framed determines much of the substance and direction of the subsequent deliberation. Throughout the process, it is important to keep in mind people's core concerns and to identify a range of potential choices that address those concerns and the issue at hand. The following guidelines can help to frame an issue effectively (McKinney and Field 2005).

- Clarify and acknowledge people's concerns.
- Group similar concerns, and take stock of the diversity of concerns and perspectives.
- Bring the problem into focus.
- Acknowledge the tensions between different perspectives.
- Map out a range of possible choices or approaches for addressing the issue.

As important as it is to name an issue in terms that bridge public concerns and values, it is equally critical to frame options in a way that encourages people who disagree with one another (or at least have different points of view) to consider and discuss their respective opinions and interests.

STEP 3: DELIBERATING ■ As a range of approaches emerges during the framing process, it is important to give people time to reflect on and discuss the benefits and drawbacks of each one. The basic question is, what do you think would happen if we tried this approach? Answering this question honestly obliges people to consider realistic consequences, to listen to the concerns and predictions of people they may disagree with, and to weigh potential cost, outcomes, and unintended side effects.

At this stage, it also helps to draw out the conflicts or tensions that arise among the different approaches. If one approach to addressing water shortages is to build more dams and reservoirs, and another is to reclaim wetlands and natural processes, the tensions may be obvious. But it is still important to ask if these approaches are mutually exclusive, or can a way be found to make them complementary? When the tensions are not so obvious, it may help to ask why it is so difficult to decide what to do about the issue. Or, if these are such good approaches, why aren't they already being implemented? In either case, the only way forward is to work through such questions, facing disagreements and conflicts in good faith, and working toward a mutually satisfying outcome.

When people confront an issue in this way—when they face difficult choices and the tradeoffs among those choices—they necessarily go beyond simple discussion or debate. Weighing the consequences of choices by working through the comparative advantages and disadvantages of each one requires deliberation.

Deliberation is collective decision making, based not on rhetoric and a glance at the headlines, but on careful consideration of other points of view, thoughtful reflection, and the public judgment of a diverse community. It often starts as a conversation among neighbors about a shared concern. If enough people recognize the concern, the dialogue may continue in letters to the editor in the local newspaper, among members of civic organizations, and in other public forums. Eventually, the conversation grows beyond personal concerns to a broader public issue and what should be done about it.

Public deliberation allows participants to frame and reframe the issue until the problem is in sharp focus. It challenges them to understand those with whom they disagree, without necessarily agreeing with them. And deliberation compels building on common ground and focusing efforts on shared goals. Finally, it drives people to act as a community. Deliberation can generate the public will that leads to "promise keeping"—the making and fulfilling of specific, practical commitments to resolve the issue. The participants themselves may promise to take action, provide funding, volunteer resources, and so on. In many cases, a deliberative public can move government to take appropriate action.

THE PRACTICE OF POLITICAL ENGAGEMENT: ROUNDTABLE ON THE CROWN OF THE CONTINENT ■ To illustrate this process of political engagement, consider the ongoing work of the Roundtable

on the Crown of the Continent. This roundtable is part of a joint effort by the Lincoln Institute of Land Policy and the Center for Natural Resources and Environmental Policy at the University of Montana (named Public Policy Research Institute until 2009) to explore how people and organizations catalyze regional initiatives and work together on large-scale, multijurisdictional landscapes. To initiate this project, the two conveners compiled an inventory of who is doing what within the region (including local, state, federal, and tribal governments; nongovernmental groups; place-based partnerships; and to a lesser extent the business community). They then convened a regional conference of about one hundred people to identify the problems and opportunities facing the region as well as promising strategies within the region and lessons learned from similar landscape-scale efforts.

After this initial step, which was designed to allow the various stakeholders to begin naming the problems in a way that made sense to most if not all people, the conveners identified leaders from different communities of interest (figure 6.3). We interviewed these leaders to clarify their individual and collective senses of the problems and opportunities facing the region (in terms of social, economic, and environmental values) and the options that might be most appropriate to address the problems and opportunities.

This intentional effort to empower multiple stakeholders to name problems and frame options jointly was captured in a short report and served as a vehicle to convene about 35 leaders from the various communities of interest in fall 2008. The focus of this gathering was to consider the various problems and options and to deliberate and search for common ground. The outcome of this effort was a consensus to continue the roundtable, seek to engage tribes and the business community in the region more effectively, and create a Web site to help define the identity and purpose of the roundtable.

DEVELOP AN ACTION PLAN

An action plan begins with the compelling issue and circumstances that brought people together. It then poses a broad hypothesis—based on the naming, framing, and deliberating process outlined above—of how to address this issue and facilitate change in the desired direction (principle 8). Most regional practitioners do not talk much about an action plan; it is

Figure 6.3
Crown of the Continent Communities of Interest

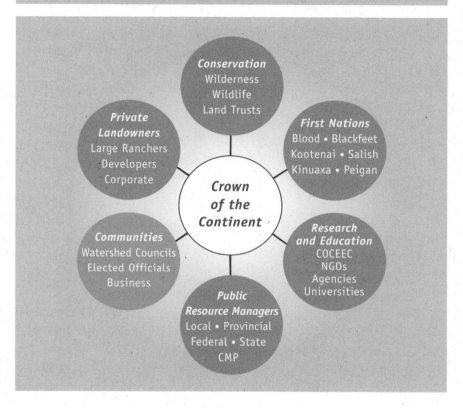

Conservation
Wilderness
Wildlife
Land Trusts

Private Landowners
Large Ranchers
Developers
Corporate

First Nations
Blood • Blackfeet
Kootenai • Salish
Kinuaxa • Peigan

Crown of the Continent

Communities
Watershed Councils
Elected Officials
Business

Research and Education
COCEEC
NGOs
Agencies
Universities

Public Resource Managers
Local • Provincial
Federal • State
CMP

implicit in the way they think and act. However, a clearly articulated action plan is important to help people see what needs to be done and to assess, improve, and adapt the plan as it unfolds.

Given the site-specific conditions of a particular regional enterprise, along with the unique needs and interests of the participants, the most effective action plans are homegrown, developed by and for the people concerned about a particular region. As illustrated by the following examples and "strategy maps," the basic idea is quite simple: clarify the context for the regional effort, summarize what you have to work with in terms of resources and capacities, agree on the problems you seek to address, specify the key strategies, and articulate what you hope to achieve in the short run and ultimately.

CALGARY REGIONAL PARTNERSHIP ■ The action plan of the Calgary Regional Partnership (CRP) is built on the premise that the best way to manage unprecedented growth in the region is to mobilize and engage the elected officials in the affected jurisdictions (figure 6.4). To accomplish this goal, CRP started small by engaging in a number of nonthreatening activities, such as improving street mapping and emergency response protocols, integrating watershed information into a regional geographic information system (GIS) program, and coordinating waste management. These activities were critical for building trust, developing working relationships, and establishing a common understanding of the social, economic, and environmental issues facing the region.

Building on these initial accomplishments, CRP then strategically formulated a common vision and set of values. This relatively nonthreatening task was critical in starting to build a sense of regional identity and led to three more tasks. First, CRP engaged the Public Policy Research Institute (PPRI) to help them negotiate a regional charter that, when complete, would establish a foundation on which to formulate a regional land use plan. PPRI staff met one-on-one with representatives from the 19 affected jurisdictions to clarify their interests and concerns. Not surprisingly, the overriding and common concern among the jurisdictions was how to think and act regionally while retaining autonomy at the local level. PPRI facilitated a series of dialogues with the elected officials and maintained a common document—which is often termed a *single negotiating text*—that captured the emerging agreement.

Second, to inform and invigorate the effort to negotiate the regional charter, CRP, in partnership with the Lincoln Institute of Land Policy, convened a two-day workshop that highlighted successful cases of regional land use planning throughout North America. The workshop, attended by more than one hundred people, also provided opportunities for the participants to develop and refine skills in regional collaboration. Among other things, this workshop demonstrated to elected officials and other participants that it is possible to balance regional goals and aspirations with local needs and interests.

For the third task, CRP engaged a number of consultants to conduct research that would demonstrate the value of working together on transboundary issues such as transportation, water supply, and wastewater treatment. As part of this research effort, CRP staff and consultants

Figure 6.4
Calgary Regional Partnership Strategy Map

Context for Our Work

The Calgary region:
- High quality of life
- Beautiful natural setting
- Strong and growing economy

A region faced with:
- Rapid growth and change
- Water supply challenges
- Significant loss of productive land due to development

What We Have to Work With

19 jurisdictions interested in strengthening relationships among elected officials across the region

Provincial interest in supporting efforts that improve planning and coordination across political boundaries

Some financial resources to support coordination efforts with the prospect for further funding for specific projects

Problems We Seek to Address

Conflicting interests and goals between urban and rural municipalities in the region

Threats to natural systems from rapid growth and development

Lack of communication and coordination across jurisdictions in the Calgary region

Increasingly complex interjurisdictional relationships and stressful annexation processes

Threats to traditional values, community identity, and political autonomy

Our Key Strategies

Develop a common vision and set of values

Start with a few small wins on interdependent issues that are easily achievable in order to build relationships and trust

Gather information from various internal and external sources in an effort to understand better the issues and challenges facing the region

Devote time and energy not only to doing projects but also to developing processes that serve to advance regional goals while preserving and honoring local differences

Develop a homegrown approach for addressing regional growth opportunities and challenges that also includes a process for mitigating and resolving conflicts between jurisdictions

What We Hope to Achieve

Short Term

Strong relationships among elected officials and their staffs from across the region

A regional charter that embodies our vision for a regional plan and represents each partner's commitment to the planning effort

Political will for regional collaboration on growth and sustainability issues

Ultimately

A high-level regional land use plan

Ongoing political will for addressing interdependent interests at the regional scale completed an inventory of existing municipal development plans and future development scenarios.

CRP's action plan is steadily building the necessary political will to develop and implement a regional land use plan. Once a preliminary plan is formulated, CRP intends to convene a series of public forums to share the ideas with citizens, business leaders, and others. CRP staff and elected officials seem to be operating on the assumption that, if the elected officials from the 19 participating jurisdictions agree, the public is likely to support the plan. Time will tell whether this strategy is effective.

CUMBERLAND REGION TOMORROW ■ The Cumberland region of middle Tennessee centers on Nashville and 13 surrounding counties. This greater metropolitan area is struggling to preserve its surprisingly rural ambience and quality of life in the face of rapid growth and the attendant development pressures, transportation tangles, and pollution problems. Because the City of Nashville is by far the largest player and holds the greatest financial and political clout, the other counties and municipalities have been reluctant to join in any formal regional planning effort for fear of being subsumed by Nashville's ambitions.

In 1999 several civic leaders convened other key players in the area to talk about the complexity of the region's issues. They realized that they needed to form a regional organization dedicated to understanding and integrating issues, information, planning tools and resources, and other people and groups at the regional level. Cumberland Region Tomorrow (CRT) was launched in 2000 to meet that need.

In the greater Nashville area, then, the action plan centers on establishing a trusted forum (CRT) in which stakeholders can identify regional-scale principles, values, and vision and seek new ways of working together to achieve interdependent interests (figure 6.5). The region's action plan hinges on a dedicated, regional-scale organization (with staff, budget, office space, and other resources) to articulate and carry out a comprehensive but focused agenda. More specifically, regional leaders see CRT as their best option for facilitating the process of building a regional identity, fostering improved relationships across jurisdictional and sectoral boundaries, and offering information, tools, and strategies that serve regional interests while maintaining local autonomy and control.

Figure 6.5
Cumberland Region Tomorrow Strategy Map

Context for Our Work

The Cumberland region:
- High quality of life
- Rich cultural heritage
- Appealing climate
- Strong and growing economy

A region faced with:
- Rapid growth
- Water quality challenges
- Traffic congestion

What We Have to Work With

An interested and engaged business community that is willing to lead a regional partnership

An iconic town (Nashville) that garners both national and international attention

Renewed public interest in living in downtown areas

Growing scientific information about conservation and water supply and quality issues

Problems We Seek to Address

Lack of coordination on growth-related issues across jurisdictional boundaries

A loss of open space and farmland, with resulting impacts on plant species, wildlife, and water quality

Inequality among subregions due to historical circumstances and ongoing incentives to compete for new development

Transportation gridlock that has resulted from significant growth and overreliance on roads, highways, and the automobile to meet transportation needs

Communications barriers among sectors with interdependent interests

Threats to sense of place and community identity

Our Key Strategies

Serve as a regional forum for discussions about land use, growth, development, and transportation issues in the Cumberland region of middle Tennessee

Provide information, planning tools, and technical assistance focused on promoting quality growth in the region, with specific focus on the following issues:

- Housing diversity
- Environment and water quality
- Economic health
- Revitalization of town centers
- Infrastructure
- Transportation
- Land use planning

Engage stakeholders across sectors in addressing regional challenges by leveraging key relationships from the private sector

What We Hope to Achieve

Short Term

A sense of regional identity

A network of committed stakeholders

Specific tools that will guide growth-related decisions in all sectors

Greater awareness of the challenges and opportunities of regional collaboration on growth-related issues

Ultimately

An integrated land use and transportation plan that embodies the quality growth principles espoused and endorsed by regional stakeholders

An ongoing capacity to identify and address regional growth challenges

CRT, in turn, is developing specific strategies aimed at reaching these near- and long-term regional goals. Staff have built a toolbox for quality growth, which provides a menu of strategies for working toward regional goals on issues like affordable housing, open space preservation, redevelopment of town centers, and transportation planning. Also, CRT strives to maintain and strengthen relationships among civic leaders to foster trust and continue to develop a shared regional identity. Ultimately, the coordination of ideas and activities through CRT will empower regional actors from all sectors to make choices that are consistent with the region's land use and transportation vision and principles.

WHAT REGIONAL INITIATIVES DO ■ As these two examples illustrate, regional initiatives may take on a number of actions depending on what they are trying to achieve. In box 6.3 the left column lists common objectives of regional initiatives, and the right column presents some typical strategies to accomplish the respective objectives. This tool is representative of the types of actions that could be included in an action plan—it is not an attempt to provide an exhaustive list of objectives or strategies.

In addition to this somewhat generic menu, several regional land use initiatives have created what might be called regional stewardship toolboxes. Cumberland Region Tomorrow, for example, created the *Quality Growth Tool Box,* which is designed to help citizens and officials implement quality growth strategies and projects in their local communities. The toolbox was developed in consultation with regional leaders, local and state agencies, and professional consultants and is meant to meet the specific needs of communities in the Cumberland region. It includes success stories, practical tools, model programs, and technical resources and support organized by theme: reinvesting in towns, city centers, and communities; creating a variety of housing choices; conserving land and other natural resources; transportation and land use planning; guiding infrastructure investments for sustainable growth; and ensuring economic vitality through quality growth.

Other examples of regional stewardship toolboxes include those developed by Envision Utah, the Cascade Agenda, Sustainable Treasure Coast in Florida, and the Great Valley Center. Once again, these are all possible resources that might inform and invigorate specific efforts to formulate an action plan. The principle here is to formulate an action plan that clarifies what you are trying to achieve and how you are going to go about it.

Box 6.3
What Regional Initiatives Do

*This tool is designed to help articulate a regional strategy map by listing some
common objectives (what needs to be done or what you are trying to achieve) along
with some common strategies (how you might go about achieving your objectives).
This list is meant to be suggestive and provocative, not comprehensive.*

What	How
Build Knowledge and Understanding	Provide public space for regional dialogue and deliberation Generate scientifically credible, politically viable, and relevant information
Build Community and Regional Identity	Inform and educate citizens and leaders Promote listening to other interests Shape public values Stimulate conversation Foster a common sense of place (a regional identity)
Frame Problems	Conduct a situation assessment Engage in research and joint fact finding Develop and monitor regional indicators Sponsor a visioning exercise Convene retreats and informal social events Create an affinity group
Discover Solutions	Convene workshops Engage in simulations and conversations (e.g., study circles, deliberative polling, citizens' juries, etc.) Provide training Learn from other regions
Implement Actions	Build on or create a precipitating event Propose pilot projects Form action teams or advocacy coalitions Prepare a communications strategy to inform and educate citizens and leaders Sponsor public events Share information through publications, Web sites, etc. Use the media to communicate the message Organize a speaker's bureau
Learn and Adapt	Document regional trends and indicators Create and maintain Web sites Establish affinity groups Recruit new participants

MOVE FROM VISION TO ACTION

Creating a regional vision and action plan requires much work, but this creative process generates many benefits (principle 9). It fosters communication, trust, and a sense of regional identity; improves people's understanding of regional issues and options for the future; builds social and political capital; and gives participants practical experience on how to work together deliberatively. In themselves, these are worthwhile accomplishments. Yet most people are interested in more than just drafting a vision or plan. They want to improve things on the ground, change policy, and build a better future. They want to move from vision to action.

Though this step may sound straightforward, many regional efforts stall at precisely this point (Cartwright and Wilbur 2005). Some of these challenges arise because of the very nature of working across boundaries. The decision-making environment is typically fragmented and lacks institutional support to work across boundaries. Also, the existing missions, mandates, and responsibilities of potential participants leave little or no time and resources for regional work. This inertia is often compounded by insufficient political will and leadership. In some cases, citizens may feel disenfranchised or apathetic, jaded by failed policies or lackluster leadership in previous efforts to address the issue at hand.

These may be serious challenges, but they can be overcome. Regional initiatives will more likely succeed in their efforts if they anticipate potential obstacles to implementation, prepare a proactive implementation strategy, and link the regional effort to formal decision-making arenas.

COMMITTING TO IMPLEMENTATION ■ Most, if not all, regional initiatives operate in environments that are less structured and more uncertain than conventional decision-making forums (such as legislatures and executive agencies). By definition, regional collaboration bridges the gaps among jurisdictions, which often have no decision-making authority of their own. When working within these gaps, then, it is critical to build a kind of "on ramp" to existing decision-making channels. Perhaps the most effective way to do this is to engage—from the very beginning—the people ultimately responsible for implementing any proposed actions.

The best strategy for moving from vision to action is to talk about action from the outset. Early in the dialogue, ask how a regional vision, plan, or agenda will be implemented. By jointly planning for implementation throughout the process, participants are less likely to waste time and resources on impractical ideas or topics that do not bring them closer to an agreeable solution. In fact, talking up front about implementation helps to keep the dialogue on track. Exploring practical options for implementing a regional agenda early in the process gives participants optimism and enthusiasm for the work ahead.

Planning for implementation throughout the process also leads to more relevant, effective outcomes. Conversely, failure to think through implementation erodes confidence and mutual trust. Without such a plan, participants may find themselves at the end of a process without a workable solution and with no recourse but to start over again, revisiting issues and redoing past work.

In some regions, it is not uncommon to find many people and groups taking action on shared issues, but not in a coordinated, collective way. Here, too, planning for implementation can help bring these fragmented efforts together under a common vision or agenda, though it may mean working back from the array of actions already taking place to a mutually agreeable set of goals and strategies for achieving them.

Despite these benefits, people often procrastinate or spend too little time on planning for implementation. They may be preoccupied with developing an agreed-upon vision or plan, rather than on determining how any outcome will be implemented. Unfortunately, even a well-intentioned effort to generate the best possible outcome may fall short if it is not sufficiently linked to the appropriate decision-making arenas, or more specifically if it does not include the people and institutions needed to implement it.

People may also trivialize the challenges of implementation. They may assume that once the "real" work of formulating a regional vision, plan, or agenda is complete, the more or less mechanical issues of implementation will take care of themselves. Too often, people rely on unrealistic assumptions about funding, the willingness of participants to take action, and the civic and political will to take action.

Sometimes people see their responsibility solely in terms of crafting a regional vision, plan, or agenda. Once the product is produced, they assume that others will put it into action. This tendency is amplified by burn out, when participants simply run out of steam. With the outcome seemingly at hand, participants may feel that they have earned the right to get back to their personal lives and let others worry about implementation.

Another obstacle is that people may avoid addressing implementation to create a "can-do" atmosphere. People who ask, "But, what if. . . ?" or "How are we going to. . . ?" are often cast as naysayers. The pressure to be positive is fine as long as the discussion about how to translate a vision, plan, or agenda into action is not buried at the never-reached bottom of the regional dialogue.

Finally, as mentioned above, inadequate attention to implementation arises when the regional effort does not engage the people who will eventually approve or implement a regional vision, plan, or agenda. Whether it is policy makers, field and line staff, constituents in the private and nongovernmental sectors, or citizens, it is critical to build awareness, understanding, and ownership among the appropriate people and institutions. The goal here is to build the civic and political will to act.

TRANSLATING VISION INTO ACTION ■ The following examples illustrate some of the key ingredients and best practices for moving from vision to action.

Envision Utah. Envision Utah is widely credited with implementing a regional land use and growth management vision for the urban corridor along the Wasatch Front east of Salt Lake City. This implementation success story is attributed to three factors: inclusiveness, values, and communication (Cartwright and Wilbur 2005).

From the outset, Envision Utah mobilized and engaged everyone who would need to play a role in implementing the regional vision: business leaders, developers, utility companies, local government, state government, conservation groups, religious leaders, educators, the media, and others. The premise was that omitting any key stakeholder would result in a missed opportunity to implement the vision.

One of the ways project leaders engaged this broad range of citizens was to interview them and ask what was most important to them. By identifying widely shared values, they reasoned, the project would create common ground and a sense of ownership or buy-in across the whole spectrum of diverse interests. Once this values analysis was complete, the leaders determined how best to accomplish the identified goals. The resulting vision spawned a growth map (figure 6.6) and a menu of strategies on how to achieve the values articulated by citizens. The overarching lesson here with respect to implementation is to identify and build on people's values (the "heart and soul" of the region) and to remove barriers to the desired future.

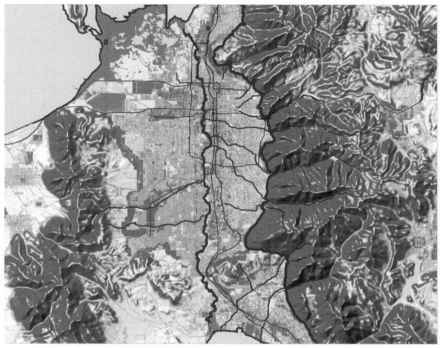

Figure 6.6
Envision Utah Growth Map

A key ingredient to the success of implementing Envision Utah's *Quality Growth Strategy* is ongoing communication. The first principle of effective communication is to package and present your message in a way that resonates with the intended audience. Envision Utah accomplished this in part by relying on professional communication experts and using a variety of communications strategies, including newspaper inserts and public service announcements.

Envision Utah's approach to creating a regional vision enjoys broad political and public support, which is vital to implementation. The state has used this strategy to formulate a long-range plan for an intermodal transportation system that will be integrated with local land use plans. Major cities are updating their land use plans to take advantage of the opportunities created by investments in the transportation system, and mayors are increasing investments in public transportation.

Regional Plan Association and the Highlands. One of the oldest regional organizations in the United States is the Regional Plan Association (RPA), an independent, nonprofit organization founded in 1922. RPA focuses on transportation, open space, and community design issues in the 31-county region centered on New York City and reaching into three states—New York, New Jersey, and Connecticut.

RPA's first planning process, in 1929, provided the blueprint for the region's transportation and open space systems. A second plan, completed in 1968, was instrumental in restoring the region's deteriorated mass transit system, preserving threatened natural resources, and revitalizing urban centers. RPA's third regional plan, released in 1996, called for improving mass transit, protecting a three-million-acre network of natural areas, preserving jobs in urban centers, and helping minorities and immigrants more fully participate in the mainstream economy.

RPA's success in implementing these plans hinges on several factors. First, RPA conducts situation assessments and holds public forums to hear from stakeholders about their values and interests on specific issues. RPA staff document widely shared values and then weigh and balance competing interests. This input directly shapes the regional vision and informs the policies and actions RPA drafts into its proposals. Press releases and newsletters provide a feedback loop so that stakeholders know that RPA listened to them.

Second, RPA routinely partners with a wide array of public and private organizations to put the plans into action. For example, to revitalize Governor's Island (in New York Harbor, just off the southern tip of Manhattan), RPA is working with the Governor's Island Preservation and Education Corporation (GIPEC), the National Park Service, and the Governor's Island Alliance—a coalition of civic, environmental, and historic preservation organizations. These partners bring technical expertise, funding, and layers of management authority to put plans and policies into place.

A third factor is RPA's sense of region and purpose, which is a good fit for its constituency. Geographically, RPA spans the parts of New York, New Jersey, and Connecticut that are inextricably tied to New York City. RPA's scope—its action plan—is broad enough to embrace distinct but related issues, such as transportation, open space, community design, and economic and cultural vitality. By focusing on these issues primarily through the lens of regional land use planning, RPA helps citizens and leaders craft a cohesive, holistic, regional vision as well as specific, practical, on-the-ground goals and projects. Both geographically and strategically, this approach embodies the wisdom behind the notion we encourage people to embrace: think regionally, act at whatever level makes the most sense.

The Highlands Conservation Act of 2004 is a good example of how diverse partners work together to implement both policy and solutions. The act is essentially an ecosystem-wide conservation plan for an environmentally rich but potentially threatened region covering 12 counties within RPA's three member states and reaching into northern Pennsylvania (figure 6.7). One in nine Americans lives within a two-hour drive of the Highlands, and the region is a direct source of quality drinking water for more than 15 million people. Approximately 1.4 million people live within the Highlands region, and another 14 million people visit the area for recreation annually.

Figure 6.7
The Highlands Region

Source: USDA Forest Service, Northeastern Area State and Private Forestry (June 2004).

The region is home to a rich variety of plant and animal life, including a number of rare and endangered species.

Despite conservation efforts dating from the early 1800s, urban and suburban sprawl has fragmented the region's forests, small farms, and open space. These changes threatened the region's drinking water quality, wildlife habitat, recreation opportunities, agricultural and forest products industries, and historic and cultural sites. During the late twentieth century, the pace of change accelerated. Population in the region has increased 11.5 percent since 1990. From 1995 to 2000, some 5,000 acres of open space per year were converted to urban uses. During this time, forested land declined annually by 3,400 acres and agriculture by 1,600 acres.

In response, a broad-based coalition built agreement on how to protect the region's natural landscapes. The coalition included people from local conservation, watershed, and open space groups; county and municipal jurisdictions; The Highlands Coalition; Regional Plan Association; The Nature Conservancy; state environmental and planning agencies; and numerous federal agencies. Their work culminated in passage of the 2004 Highlands Conservation Act. Under provisions of the act, the U.S. Forest Service now works with local jurisdictions and interested people to identify lands that have high conservation value in the Highlands areas of Connecticut, New York, New Jersey, and Pennsylvania. Each year, governors of these four states may submit land conservation projects in the Highlands for funding not to exceed 50 percent of the total cost.

The RPA story echoes many of the lessons of regional collaboration: provide for inclusive participation; focus on common values; rely on diverse strategies to meet agreed-upon goals; and create a link to formal decision-making arenas. This case also suggests one additional, very important ingredient to the implementation of regional visions, plans, and agendas: foster a sustained commitment over a long period of time.

CALFED Bay-Delta Program.   Regional governance is not always a resounding success. The emphasis on governance sometimes results in statutory mandates for regionalism and collaboration that are not grounded in the best interests of the region.

The California Bay-Delta hydrologic region centers on the delta of the Sacramento and San Joaquin rivers flowing into San Francisco Bay (figure

6.8). This system provides drinking water for 22 million people and irriga-
tion water for a $27 billion agricultural industry. Its levees protect farms,
homes, and infrastructure. It is the largest estuary on the West Coast of the
United States and supports 80 percent of California's commercial salmon
fishery. Straining under dual roles as crucial habitat and water project
crossroads, the Bay-Delta suffers from decades of competing demands. It
no longer functions as a healthy ecosystem or as a reliable source of water.

In 1994 several state and federal agencies began an ambitious regional
partnership known as the
CALFED Bay-Delta Pro-
gram. Over the next five
years, cooperating agen-
cies worked with stake-
holders and the public to
develop a 30-year plan to
restore the ecosystem and
improve water supply reliability, water quality, and
levee system integrity.
The cooperating agencies
issued a record of decision
in 2000, and in 2003 the
California Bay-Delta Act
established the California
Bay-Delta Authority as the
new governance structure
for the program. Congress
approved the record of decision as a general framework
and authorized nonvoting
participation of the authority in October 2004.

The 24-member
authority operates in a
highly structured, for-
mal governance arena.

Figure 6.8
The California Bay-Delta

Source: CALFED Science Program
(http://science.calwater.ca.gov/pdf/psp/PSP_2006_Fig1B_Bay-Delta_063006.pdf).

It is comprised of state and federal agency representatives, public members, a member of the Bay-Delta Public Advisory Board, ex officio legislative members, and members at large. It is charged to improve the quality and reliability of California's water supplies while restoring the Bay-Delta ecosystem. Among its tasks are providing accountability, ensuring balanced implementation, tracking and assessing program progress, using sound science, assuring public involvement and outreach, and coordinating and integrating related government programs.

According to a recent evaluation of the authority's performance by the Little Hoover Commission—a bipartisan, independent state agency that promotes efficiency and effectiveness in state programs—"[t]he vision is not flawed, but the implementation effort has drifted off course" (Little Hoover Commission 2005, ii). The program "has demonstrated the propensity for rudderless bureaucracies to get caught in inescapable eddies" (Little Hoover Commission 2005, i). Among the problems cited by the commission are major disagreements between agencies and among stakeholders that have slowed or stalled progress and the dilution of leadership responsibility when it passed from the state secretary of resources to the authority. "One lesson from the CALFED experiment is that process and structure cannot substitute for leadership or authority" (Little Hoover Commission 2005, iii).

The report also notes that CALFED was designed around four principles: (1) good communication; (2) active and effective involvement of stakeholders; (3) reliance on science to make decisions; and, (4) sustained and personal leadership. "Most of the current problems can be traced back to violations—even brief ones—of those principles" (Little Hoover Commission 2005, ii).

The evaluation by the Little Hoover Commission concluded that the governance design of the authority does not provide the right carrots and sticks to ensure coordination across jurisdictions and agencies. Consequently, while some agency officials and stakeholders are working more closely together (and some fish populations are stabilized and showing signs of rebounding), there have been recent declines in other ecological values, and the delta's water supplies are only marginally more reliable.

The report presents several ways to improve implementation, which are paraphrased below. These would apply well to implementing any regional vision, plan, or agenda.

- Define specifically what CALFED will accomplish and how it will achieve those goals.
- Identify a collaborative leader and give that person clear authority and consolidated responsibility.
- Create the right incentives for multiple jurisdictions and agencies to work together. Mandating collaboration rarely, if ever, works.
- Foster public support (or civic will) by providing more meaningful and effective opportunities for citizens and stakeholders to be involved.

CONCLUSION

While formulating a regional vision, plan, or agenda is an important step, it is only one step among many. Regional practitioners must also articulate the steps that need to be taken (and who will take them) to ensure that their efforts will be implemented (box 6.4).

If the intent of a regional initiative is to propose legislation, create a new administrative program, establish cooperative initiatives among multiple agencies or organizations, or conduct research, the fundamental challenge is how to link the proposed actions to the appropriate arena for implementation. In some cases, participants will need to work closely with elected and appointed officials who can ratify recommendations. In other cases, regional practitioners will need to create coalitions with the private, nongovernmental, and university sectors to get things done.

The most important strategy for addressing this challenge is to engage the agencies and people responsible for implementation from the very beginning. They can spell out legal and policy constraints and priorities and help participants focus on solutions that are achievable. Early involvement also allows those agencies to develop a sense of ownership and commitment to any proposed outcome, thereby increasing their willingness to accept responsibility for implementation.

The process of regional collaboration must not only provide a platform to articulate an action plan. It must also create some certainty that the actions will be carried out to achieve the desired outcomes. Without some clear indication that the results of the process will have teeth, the incentive to participate is greatly diminished. The key to translating regional visions into actions is to develop an implementation plan as part of the overall action plan, not as an afterthought.

Box 6.4
Seven Habits for Effective Implementation

These case studies, combined with the literature on collaboration and public policy implementation, suggest seven habits for effective implementation of regional visions, plans, and agendas.

1. Think regionally and act at whatever level makes sense.

In years past, the mantra of regionalists was to "think and act regionally" (McKinney, Parr, and Seltzer 2004). Practical experience, however, suggests that sometimes the best way to achieve a regional vision, plan, or agenda is to act at the scale that affords the most traction. In other words, the vision may be regional in scope, but much of the work to accomplish that vision is done at the neighborhood, community, county, or other jurisdictional level.

2. Anticipate the challenges of implementating regional strategies.

As a range of regional strategies arises during the process of articulating an action plan, it is important to give people time to reflect on and discuss the benefits and drawbacks of each approach. The basic question is, What do you think would happen if we tried this approach? Answering this question should reveal two things: how effective a particular strategy is likely to be if implemented; and how likely implementation is. Several additional questions are useful to forecast implementation problems.

- Are the regional objectives communicated clearly? Are they precise, consistent with each other, prioritized, and ranked relative to other agendas?
- What operational demands will the regional vision, plan, or agenda make? What is the nature of the service or function? How will it affect existing public, private, and nongovernmental actors? How difficult will it be to control the regional agenda?
- Are the resources—money, personnel, authority, information, supplies and equipment, and space—adequate to implement the regional vision, plan, or agenda?
- What are the consequences of sharing responsibility across jurisdictions, agencies, and sectors? How will the many actors needed for implementation affect the likelihood of implementation given different missions, mandates, and incentives?

Box 6.4
(continued)

■   Finally, if this regional vision, plan, or agenda is such a good idea, why is it not being implemented already?

Taken together, these diagnostic questions oblige regional stewards to consider realistic consequences, to listen to the concerns and predictions of people they may disagree with, and to weigh the potential costs, outcomes, and unintended side effects. Addressing these types of questions leads to a more viable action plan, and also helps people generate the will to take action, provide funding, organize volunteer resources, and otherwise help implement the action plan.

3. Develop an implementation schedule as part of your regional action plan.
Having identified the challenges to implementation, regional practitioners should then develop an implementation schedule that includes clear, specific statements of what needs to be done, how it will be accomplished, when the results are needed and expected, and who is responsible for what.

This schedule should provide a road map showing how to overcome the challenges of implementation along with a very explicit mechanism for holding the participants to their commitments. In this respect, the schedule of implementation provides performance measures—that is, objective means to track the commitment of individual parties and the overall performance of implementing the agreement.

An implementation schedule includes first deciding what needs to be done and by what date, and then identifying the person responsible. The participants should inventory their collective assets and determine who should do what. Some people may have better contacts with key decision makers, while others might be more effective at working with the people in the private sector or with the general public. The goal here is to employ the resources of all the participants to translate the regional vision into action. For large or complex regional initatives, it is best to document the implementation schedule in a written implementation plan.

4. Seek ratifaction among relevant constituencies.
Once a regional coalition has crafted an action plan, anticipated implementation challenges, and prepared an implementation plan, the participants need

Box 6.4
(continued)

to seek ratification. They should confirm the proposal with their constituents, address any issues that emerged, and make an individual commitment to the regional vision, plan, or agenda. In most cases, participants should ratify their commitment in writing. Such a rite of ownership helps to solidify buy-in and also provides a written record to return to as needed if people try to recant.

5. Clarify participants' personal commitment to the regional vision, plan, or agenda.

Not all of the participants in a regional dialogue represent a larger constituency, and even if they do they may not have the authority to speak for the stakeholders they supposedly represent. Nevertheless, it is appropriate to ask each individual to indicate their personal support by signing an agreement. Such statements typically declare that the people who sign not only support the package of recommendations being presented, but also promise to work to implement the various proposed actions (and to follow through on any commitment they may have made). If appropriate, the statement may include a sentence to the effect that signatories have in fact consulted their constituencies and received their endorsement.

6. Present the regional vision, plan, or agenda to key decision makers and leaders in the public, private, and nongovernment sectors.

Given that most regional initiatives supplement existing decision-making processes, it is absolutely critical to create a link or bridge between informal and formal decision-making bodies. In short, regional practitioners must take account of existing processes—political, legal, regulatory, and so on—and build the political and civic will to take action. What works best at this stage is to seek access to power (rather than power itself) by building bridges, coordinating actions, and completing the mundane but important tasks that would otherwise be left undone.

Regional practitioners should start by understanding how the proposed regional action supplements other relevant efforts. Then they need to communicate their message to appropriate audiences, making it relevant and compelling. They should explain how the group arrived at its recommended action plan and make themselves available to answer questions about the content of

Box 6.4
(continued)

the proposal and the process of formulating the plan. They need to demonstrate to political leaders and other decision makers that the political capital to be gained is greater than any political risk they may take in supporting the action.

In the final analysis, regional practitioners should ask those with authority to act to indicate their reaction to the proposed regional vision, plan, or agenda, and to describe the steps they intend to take to follow through on what has been proposed.

7. Celebrate progress and monitor implementation.

Implementing a regional vision, plan, or agenda takes time. The goal is to catalyze incremental change throughout the region and to do this by "building momentum toward a tipping-point" (Cartwright and Wilbur 2005, 5). Given this long-term proposition, it is important to do two things (both of which are addressed in the next chapter).

First, recognize and celebrate the progress that is made along the way and the people who have made a difference. Second, create a team that can periodically report back to other participants on progress. In some cases, it may be necessary to reconvene the participants if those in authority are not willing to implement the proposed actions to see what changes might be possible. In other cases, the accomplishments and successes may be so significant that they warrant a celebration, bringing together the people who made it happen to thank them for their efforts and raising broader public awareness of the initiative through favorable media attention.

Chapter 7

EVALUATE, LEARN, AND ADAPT

As the process of implementing a regional action plan unfolds, it is important to evaluate whether the work is achieving the desired outcomes and determine how to proceed. Evaluation includes two activities: monitoring and measuring progress. Monitoring is simply tracking what happens as the plan unfolds. A good monitoring program documents how the world changes as specific actions ripple across the region. Monitoring also reveals whether regional participants are fulfilling the roles and responsibilities to which they agreed. Measuring progress builds on the information gleaned from monitoring. It focuses on whether a regional effort is having the desired effect. Careful monitoring and measuring enable participants to evaluate whether the action plan should be modified in response to new information or changing conditions (Susskind and Cruikshank 2006; Yaffee et al. 2004).

When working across boundaries, evaluation is a process of "civic learning" (Mathews 2005). People with diverse interests jointly observe the effects of their collective actions and learn, together, from that experience (principle 10). As such, evaluation helps participants build a common understanding of how their collaboration affects the issue at hand. It also provides political momentum for regional participants to follow through on difficult problems and to transfer hard-won social, political, and intellectual capital from one project to the next. The operative principle here is to learn together as you go forward and adapt as needed.

CAPTURE AND COMMUNICATE PROGRESS

There are three primary reasons to capture and communicate the progress of regional initiatives. The first is to improve the desired outcomes of a regional vision, plan, or agenda. Research on ecosystem management and community-based collaboration strongly suggests that regional initiatives are much more likely to meet their objectives when they set clear goals, monitor implementation, learn from their experience, and adapt their strategies accordingly (McKinney and Field 2008; Yaffee et al. 2004).

Evaluating progress enables participants to use the resulting information to identify the strengths and weaknesses of the action plan; clarify which elements work or do not work and why; and renew, revise, and adapt the action plan accordingly. It also helps in addressing emergent issues and concerns of the participants and others. This process of learning by doing, or adaptive management, not only fosters higher levels of success in the face of inevitable uncertainty and change, but also creates a culture of civic learning. It enhances the collective ability to do better next time and leads to greater accountability and clearer roles and responsibilities. It also helps to maximize the impact of limited resources (Brunner et al. 2005; Lee 1993; Scholz and Stiftel 2005).

The second reason to evaluate progress is to demonstrate and communicate success. Creating the capacity to share the success of a regional initiative can build and maintain support among citizens and officials for implementation. It can also be a very effective means to recruit and engage new people. In addition, the results of an evaluation can improve opportunities for funding by showing potential donors how the regional effort is doing positive things that would not otherwise get done.

The third reason to monitor and evaluate the progress of a regional initiative is to determine whether or not it should continue. Some regional initiatives emerge, take action, and intentionally dissolve. There is no interest in continuing or reason to do so. In other situations, regional practitioners may have no intention of creating an ongoing platform for regional dialogue and action, but their initial success may provide the evidence and motivation needed to continue.

Evaluating a regional initiative can help determine if there is a need to continue. It can provide the information required to move beyond individual instances of success to long-range, programmatic accomplishments; build the necessary capacities required to be sustainable and effective; and move from an informal to a formal regional organization.

Evaluating progress adds value to short-term, ad hoc regional efforts. It also lights the way ahead for initiatives that are exploring the value of transitioning from an informal to a more formal enterprise. Longstanding regional organizations can revitalize and refine their efforts based on timely, honest evaluation of their work to date.

Given this range of benefits, why do some regions skip this step? Some regional coalitions may feel that conducting an evaluation is a waste of scarce resources that would be better invested in actually doing something. Others may feel threatened by the idea of evaluation, which to them implies a negative judgment about the efficacy of their work. Still other regional groups may not be able to agree on a clear set of regional objectives and are thus unable to evaluate progress. Some simply lack the capacity to collect data and complete the analysis or have never thought about evaluation.

The process of monitoring and evaluating regional efforts can be either short and simple, or it can be complex and take significant time and resources. To stay short of the point of diminishing returns, it is important to tailor monitoring and evaluation to the specific needs and interests of the region; build the mechanisms for monitoring and evaluation into your action plan from the outset, not as an afterthought; and keep a running file of feedback, including unsolicited praise or complaints and any media publicity. Another timesaver is using existing information: for example, tally total project hours from staff and volunteer timesheets, cite newspaper and television coverage of regional accomplishments, or use sign-in sheets at open houses and workshops to estimate participation in regional events.

What happens when regional practitioners do not monitor and evaluate their progress? They spend precious time and money doing things that may not lead to the desired outcome. They may actually be doing many good things, but no one knows about them, thereby limiting the effectiveness and sustainability of the regional effort. Finally, regional practitioners may lose their sense of purpose and direction if they do not periodically take a candid look at their progress.

EVALUATE OUTCOMES AND PROCESS

Despite the growing interest in evaluating collaborative processes of all types, including regional collaboration, the standards vary widely (McKinney and Field 2008). Some observers argue that collaboration should be evaluated against the goals and aspirations of the participants. Others claim that evaluation should focus on whether collaboration does a better job than alternative processes. The idea here is to compare collaboration against its real-world alternatives and assess what would most likely happen if there were no regional collaboration. Still other critics suggest that collaboration should be evaluated against some idealistic theory about participatory democracy, regional governance, or another relevant theory or preconceived outcome (for example, did collaboration improve the environment?).

The most practical approach is to focus on methods to evaluate the progress of particular projects or programs and clarify the key ingredients to success. This approach assumes that participants are in the best position to evaluate the relative success of their effort (Susskind and Cruikshank 1987). However, not everyone agrees with this premise. Coglianese (2003), for example, argues that participant satisfaction is not an important or meaningful goal because not all of the people affected by a policy decision are included in the evaluation, and thus participant satisfaction provides only a partial representation of social welfare. He goes on to claim that participant satisfaction is a relatively meaningless measure of success because the fact that people are satisfied with a policy decision or outcome does not necessarily mean that it is a good one.

We agree that this approach to evaluation creates some selection bias because it does not include the views of people who are not part of a particular collaborative effort but who may nevertheless be interested in and affected by the outcomes. To mitigate this limitation, it is possible to include in an evaluation some questions about the degree to which the process was open to anyone who wanted to participate and the degree of accountability to the general public.

Most theories and methods of evaluation suggest that it is valuable to measure both outcome and process factors (Leach 2004; Macfarlane and Mayer n.d.; and Weber 2003). While the synthesis in box 7.1 provides a useful orientation, it is important

Box 7.1
Evaluating Outcomes and Process

Evaluating Outcomes
- Did you (or are you) achieving your objectives or interests?
- Are you doing better than your best alternative to regional collaboration?
- Are the outcomes wise? Are they based on the best possible information?
- Can the outcomes be implemented? Are they politically, technically, and financially feasible?

Evaluating Process
- Did everyone who wanted to participate have a meaningful opportunity to do so?
- Was the process efficient relative to your alternatives?
- Did you learn something from the experience? (intellectual capital)
- Did people build trust and relationships? (social and political capital)

to keep in mind that the most useful indicators to monitor and evaluate will vary from region to region. Figure 7.1 presents one of the most effective frameworks to evaluate projects and programs in general, including regional collaboration (Yaffee et al. 2004).

Evaluation is not linear but iterative, an ongoing process to help participants do better. As Yaffee notes, "information gained from the process can be used to begin the process again with more clarity and effectiveness" (Yaffee et al. 2004, 7). Regardless of the specific approach employed

Figure 7.1
The Evaluation Cycle

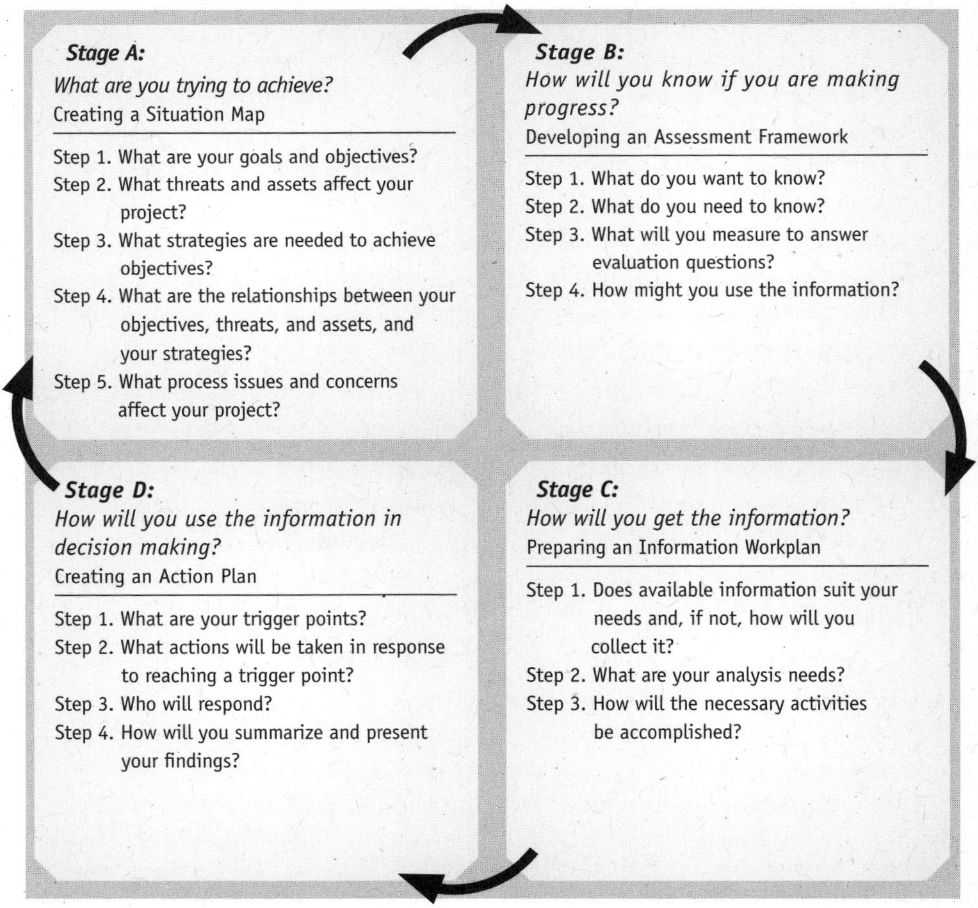

Stage A:
What are you trying to achieve?
Creating a Situation Map

Step 1. What are your goals and objectives?
Step 2. What threats and assets affect your project?
Step 3. What strategies are needed to achieve objectives?
Step 4. What are the relationships between your objectives, threats, and assets, and your strategies?
Step 5. What process issues and concerns affect your project?

Stage B:
How will you know if you are making progress?
Developing an Assessment Framework

Step 1. What do you want to know?
Step 2. What do you need to know?
Step 3. What will you measure to answer evaluation questions?
Step 4. How might you use the information?

Stage D:
How will you use the information in decision making?
Creating an Action Plan

Step 1. What are your trigger points?
Step 2. What actions will be taken in response to reaching a trigger point?
Step 3. Who will respond?
Step 4. How will you summarize and present your findings?

Stage C:
How will you get the information?
Preparing an Information Workplan

Step 1. Does available information suit your needs and, if not, how will you collect it?
Step 2. What are your analysis needs?
Step 3. How will the necessary activities be accomplished?

Source: Yaffee et al. (2003).

to monitor and evaluate progress, implementation can be improved by considering the four key questions in this general framework along with maintaining a focus on both process and outcome factors.

The information generated by evaluation also can be used to document and celebrate success and to capture and transfer lessons. Celebrating success can take many forms, from special events, to giving awards, to recognition from prominent civic leaders or politicians (Parr, Walesh, and Nguyen 2002). Documenting and celebrating successes also allow groups to recognize what has gone well, from strengthening relationships to accomplishing specific programmatic tasks to building a stronger sense of community and place. This step can be particularly valuable when there are new regional partners, or when the leadership of an initiative changes, so that core processes and lessons learned can be shared quickly.

Given the variety of regional experiments and approaches used to evaluate progress, three approaches—scorecards, objective indicators, and reports—are discussed, moving from lower-cost to higher-cost methods.

Evaluating Regional Collaboration is a participant satisfaction scorecard (see Appendix) that provides an efficient and effective way to evaluate the progress of regional collaboration. The scorecard includes a Likert scale list of 27 indicators of success synthesized from the literature and practical experience. It allows participants to evaluate the outcomes of regional collaboration, the effects on working relationships, and the quality of the process itself. It also allows participants to reflect on the value of regional collaboration relative to alternatives available to a particular region.

The Consensus Building Institute used a version of the Evaluating Regional Collaboration scorecard to evaluate 50 cases of community-based collaboration (CBC) on federal lands and resources in the Rocky Mountain West (McKinney and Field 2008). Seventy percent of the respondents said that all 27 indicators were important contributors to their satisfaction with the process and its outcomes. Eighty-six percent of the participants stated they would recommend a CBC process to address a similar issue in the future, a strong indicator of people's satisfaction with the process and its outcomes. More specifically, the respondents indicated that CBC improved working relationships among the participants; facilitated a process that was open to and inclusive of all interests, viewpoints, and stakeholders; fostered informed decision making; and was efficient in terms of time and money, particularly when compared to the alternatives. The bottom line was that 72 percent of respondents said that CBC produced a more effective, lasting outcome over their next-best alternative.

As a tool or method for evaluating regional collaboration, the Evaluating Regional Collaboration scorecard does have some limitations. First, it does not include the views of people who are not part of a particular regional effort, but who nevertheless may be interested in and affected by the outcomes. Although it includes a number of questions about the degree to which the regional process was open to anyone who wanted to participate and the degree of accountability to the public, it is important to keep in mind that it is only a partial representation of social welfare or the overall value of regional collaboration.

Second, this scorecard does not attempt to evaluate the on-the-ground improvement of social, economic, environmental, or other outcomes. It does not presume that one outcome, such as environmental protection or economic development, is necessarily better than another. As explained above, that is a judgment to be made by the participants.

To measure on-the-ground impacts, regional practitioners might consider a second approach—the use of more objective indicators. According to the Alliance for Regional Stewardship, indicators are used to measure trends in social, economic, and environmental systems and to help people see the bigger picture through small details (Carrier and Wallis 2005). Indicators measure what a region looks like and how it changes over time. Increasingly, many regions throughout the country are turning to indicators as a way to measure their progress on these issues. While the technical information presented in indicator reports is useful to analysts and decision makers, it can also be a very useful way to foster regional identity, raise awareness and understanding, and mobilize and engage people around regional land use, natural resource, and environmental issues.

Based on a study of 25 different regional indicator projects, which included a total of 250 indicators, the alliance created a matrix of commonly used indictors (Carrier and Wallis 2005). Twenty-four indicators were used in more than 50 percent of the projects, while only one indicator (having to do with home affordability and median home price) was used in more than 90 percent of the projects (box 7.2). Five additional indicators (population trends, crime rates, unemployment rate, transit ridership, and air quality) were used in more than 75 percent of the projects.

Box 7.2

Regional Indicators Matrix Summary

Demographic Indicators

Population trends were used in 20 projects (80 percent), and ethnicity/age diversity was used in 16 (64 percent).

Economic Indicators for Business Vitality

No indicators in this category were used in more than 7 projects (28 percent).

Economic Indicators for Employment and Income

Within this category, a large number of indicators were used frequently.

- Unemployment rate (seasonal)—used 19 times (76 percent).
- Job growth/labor force growth/employment trends overall (high- and low-paying industries), labor force participation rate—used 18 times (72 percent).
- Employment by sector/industry cluster (technology/nontechnology), public/private sector (top sectors by gain/loss) (by city)—used 18 times (72 percent).
- Poverty (adult/children/families/seniors) (geographic concentration)—used 16 times (64 percent).
- Job growth (loss) by sector/industry cluster (technology/nontechnology), diversification—used 15 times (60 percent).
- Average/median household/family income—used 15 times (60 percent).
- Average hourly/annual wages (also for farm workers compared to other workers), growth in real wages (clusters versus nonclusters, technology versus nontechnology)—used 13 times (52 percent).

Economic Indicators for Technology and Innovation

No indicators in this category were used in more than 9 projects (36 percent).

Economic Indicators for Working Landscapes

The indicator named "acres of open space/protected open space (includes farms as well as major protected habitats), land at risk, land trust holdings" was used 13 times (52 percent).

Economic Indicators for Housing and Urban Land Use

The most commonly used indicator in all the reports, "Affordability Index (percent who can purchase median-priced home, households spending 35 percent or more on

Box 7.2
(continued)

housing, income required for median-priced home), median home price/value," was used 24 times (96 percent).

Additionally, the following indicators were used frequently:

- Urban footprint—extent of urbanization, population density, rate of undeveloped land conversion for urban uses, efficient land reuse—used 16 times (64 percent).
- Rental Affordability Index (by income, households spending 30–35 percent or more on housing), rental rates, vacancy rates, hourly wage needed—used 16 times (64 percent).

Economic Indicators for Transportation and Mobility

- Transit ridership (passenger bus, commuter rail, demand response)—used 19 times (76 percent).
- Average commute time/commute speed—used 15 times (60 percent).

Social Indicators for Education and Training

- SAT performance of students, School Academic Performance Index, Similar School Rank—used 16 times (64 percent).
- High school drop out/attrition rate, graduation rate—used 13 times (52 percent).

Social Indicators for Young Children and Families

None of the indicators in this category was used in more than 9 projects (36 percent).

Social Indicators for Health, Human Services, and Public Safety

- Violent and property crime/arrest rates—used 20 times (80 percent).
- Health status (mortality rates, causes of death, communicable diseases, chronic diseases, suicide rate)—used 14 times (56 percent).

Environmental Indicators for Natural Resources

One indicator, "urban footprint—extent of urbanization, population density, rate of undeveloped land conversion for urban uses, efficient land reuse," was used 14 times (56 percent).

Environmental Indicators for Air and Water Quality/Use, Energy, Solid Waste

- Days in violation of federal/state air quality standards, bad air days, ozone exposure—used 19 times (76 percent).
- Per capita water usage, urban water usage—used 14 times (56 percent).
- Solid waste generated/recycled/diversion—used 14 times (56 percent).

Civic Engagement Indicators: Citizenship, Community Participation, and Culture

One indicator, "voter participation of registered/eligible voters," was used 16 times (64 percent).

Source: Carrier and Wallis (2005).

Building on the use of indicators, a third approach to measuring regional progress is to create a state-of-the-region report. Highlighting the most relevant factors (such as some of the indicators described above), such a report presents a narrative that tracks the region's progress, communicates successes, and plans for the future.

Based on the premise "you can't manage what you can't measure," the University of Buffalo Regional Institute (1999) completed the first state-of-the-region report to monitor the region's performance in key areas. This effort is typical of most state-of-the-region progress reports. By providing objective and timely data on critical issues, the project serves as a reliable base of information to guide policy action and encourage long-range planning in this binational, multijurisdictional region.

The *California Regional Progress Report* is notable because it provides a common framework and set of indicators to measure regional progress statewide (California Center for Regional Leadership 2007). The intent is to inform state, regional, and local decision makers about transportation, housing, land use, environmental resources, and other infrastructure concerns. The annual report is part of the California Regional Blueprint Planning Program, an initiative of the state legislature to provide funding to metropolitan planning organizations, councils of government, and other regional bodies to conduct regional scenario planning as a way to improve land use and transportation systems into the future. This initiative, and the annual progress report, recognizes that California's regions are unique: each deals with a different set of demographic, economic, environmental, and other assets and challenges. Thus, while the report tracks a common set of indicators across all regions, it also monitors and evaluates how individual regions are progressing compared to their past performance and desired outcomes.

The annual *State of the Rockies Report Card* covers the multistate region of the Rocky Mountain West. This report and an associated conference, sponsored by Colorado College (n.d.), provide a comprehensive and accessible statement about the challenges and controversies facing the eight Rocky Mountain states. The report card provides communities, local governments, and business leaders with a complete and regular assessment of their local assets while fostering an integrated understanding of the dynamic changes occurring in the region. First published in 2004, the report card has tracked and evaluated indicators related to economic growth and decay, energy use, habitat conservation, cultural development, and civic engagement.

DETERMINE IF THERE IS A NEED TO CONTINUE

Every regional initiative eventually finds itself at a decision point to determine whether to continue or disband. Typically, the dilemma is framed as, Is our work done? or, Our work is done—now what? These questions bring us full circle to the first principle of working across boundaries: focus on a compelling purpose or interest. In short, is there a compelling reason to continue? Revisiting the original goals of the regional initiative allows participants to determine whether those conditions still exist, and whether that work still needs to be done. Alternatively, there may be reasons to expand or change the scope of the initiative to encompass new compelling issues and interests.

The same set of tools and diagnostic questions presented in chapter 4 to help determine whether to begin regional collaboration can help answer the question of whether to continue or disband. A few additional questions may also help in making this decision.

■ Has the regional initiative accomplished all that it set out to do?
■ Is anything left undone that needs to be addressed?

- If the regional initiative disbanded tomorrow, what would happen?
  - What good things might happen? (Do other people now have the capacity to collaborate regionally without the initiative's support?)
  - What bad things might happen? (Would the problem recur, would needs go unmet, or would opportunities go unanswered?)

Sometimes the decision to continue or sunset a regional initiative is made at the outset as a prerequisite of working together. If preexisting working relationships and trust are weak, stakeholders may insist that the group limit its scope to the issue at hand. Some collaborative efforts make this a condition of the ground rules—when the agreed-upon work is completed, or if no agreeable solution can be found within a reasonable time, the group will disband. Stakeholders may prefer this approach because it limits their responsibility to one specific issue and a defined timeframe. Or they may prefer it because they are wary of any unbounded process that might lead to a new layer of bureaucracy and expense.

In other cases, stakeholders may agree from the outset that the catalyzing issue is an ongoing one that is not likely to go away. They may agree that a longer-term or permanent effort is the only investment worth making. People prefer this approach when they realize that an ongoing regional initiative is the best way to secure their interests.

Strategies for monitoring and measuring progress can also be designed early on in the process to help determine whether to continue or disband a regional initiative. For example, benchmarks for desired outcomes can serve as a checklist to ensure that no needs are left unmet, no work undone. If such benchmarks have not been checked off, then it would be premature to disband. Similarly, if the evaluation process reveals that some tools or strategies have been less than effective, issues that need to be addressed may remain. Finally, disbanding a loosely formed network or informal partnership is usually less complicated than dismantling a more formal regional arrangement, such as an incorporated regional organization or regional governance structure. But in any case, the move should be made with the same attention to openness, transparency, inclusiveness, and deliberation that characterized the collaboration in the first place. The choice to continue or disband a regional initiative is not a one-time decision point, but more likely a recurring crossroads.

BUILD THE CAPACITY TO SUSTAIN

Assuming that people see value in continuing their initiative, they must then build the capacity to sustain their effort. In the near term, this means focusing on the essential ingredients of any such effort—funds, people, and civic support—to continue the work at hand. To sustain a regional initiative, it is important to revisit these ingredients periodically and ferret out any gaps, unmet needs, or missed opportunities.

Sustaining work across boundaries over a longer term—perhaps indefinitely—requires a bit more work. Before investing the necessary time and energy in moving forward, participants should revisit, deliberate on, and recommit to the principles that guided them to this point (figure 7.2). The aim here is not to belabor the decisions made at the outset, but to assess progress, adapt to any changes in the region, and plan and prepare the most effective way forward.

Reviewing all of the principles and elements can lead to improvements in the action plan and on-the-ground implementation. In themselves, such improvements can help sustain a regional initiative. But it is also important to consider how the principles apply in a long-term context. In the case of leadership, for example, it is crucial to have homegrown leaders with collaborative skills and values. A few such leaders may be available in the region for immediate, short-term issues. But over the course of years or decades, collaborative leadership must be developed and nurtured through leadership seminars, mentoring, and succession planning. Thinking 20 years or more down the road puts each of the principles in a different light.

- The initial catalyst becomes a clear, compelling mission statement.
- Engaging the right people becomes securing their long-term commitment.
- Defining the region becomes building and refining a strong sense of regional identity.
- Organizing around collaborative leaders becomes developing and mentoring such leaders and planning for succession in each sector of the region.
- Assembling resources and building capacity become diversifying sources (particularly of funding) and providing a home for capacity to take root.
- An action plan becomes an ongoing campaign and business plan.

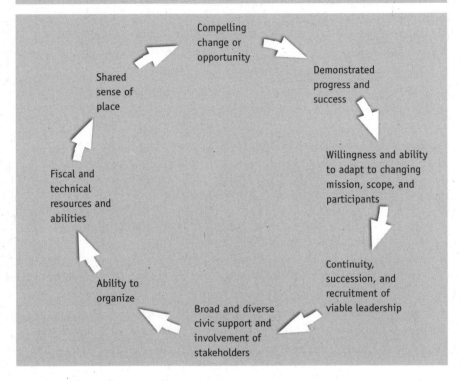

Figure 7.2
What Sustains Regional Collaboration?

Compelling change or opportunity

Demonstrated progress and success

Willingness and ability to adapt to changing mission, scope, and participants

Continuity, succession, and recruitment of viable leadership

Broad and diverse civic support and involvement of stakeholders

Ability to organize

Fiscal and technical resources and abilities

Shared sense of place

- Implementation continues, but also includes management and perhaps operation and maintenance.
- Evaluation leads to ongoing adaptation and refinement.

Applying the core principles over the long term points to a tendency for regional initiatives to become more formally organized as they mature. This does not mean that networks and partnerships morph into some sort of regional institution, although that occasionally does happen. More likely, the underlying structure remains essentially the same, while operating protocols and working relationships are refined and, to some extent, codified.

In the Crown of the Continent, for example, seven years after its inception the Crown of the Continent Ecosystem Managers Partnership remains a voluntary partnership. But in its sixth year, the participants jointly drafted and adopted a strategic plan complete with vision and mission statements, guiding principles and shared values, and articulated goals. The plan also outlines the partnership's organizational structure centered on a steering committee and secretariat. This arrangement allows participating federal, state, provincial, and tribal agencies to coordinate policies and management activities while remaining independent and faithful to their individual missions and mandates.

The Stewardship Network in Michigan also began as an informal partnership. In 1995, three local conservation groups met to explore ways to manage open space and natural areas in a more coordinated, holistic way. In 1998, they launched the Huron River Watershed Volunteer Stewardship Network, which was aimed primarily at growing a network of conservation volunteers. The network formed a broad-based advisory committee of stakeholders across the region, partnering with watershed councils, land conservancies, city parks departments, and local schools and universities. This led to more diverse, sustainable streams for funding and partnerships and a gradual expansion of geographic scope to include all of Michigan.

The Stewardship Network incorporated as a 501(c)(3) nonprofit in 2004 with a well-developed organizational structure that features a central office and seven stewardship clusters around the state. It is governed by an 11-member board of directors, with program guidance from a smaller program committee. Informal partnerships with dozens of other organizations around the state continue to be an integral part of how the network achieves its goals.

The Regional Plan Association is an example of an ad hoc group that formalized into a permanent, carefully structured regional institution. RPA traces its roots to the Committee on a Regional Plan for New York and its Environs, formed in 1922. The committee produced a regional plan in 1929, the same year that it was incorporated as a permanent organization to implement the plan and to develop new plans as needed. Today, RPA is governed by a 60-member board of directors from three states. A president and professional staff oversee daily operations and a budget of $4.4 million.

These examples highlight several critical features that help to make a regional initiative sustainable—secure funding, administrative capacity, and clearly articulated operating protocols designed for the long term.

Funding for a regional effort often starts with a little seed money and a great deal of volunteer labor, but these are not enough to sustain work over years or decades. More secure funding sources, such as grants and donations, are required over time. In most cases, multiple sources provide a more sustainable funding stream than a single source. One advantage of working across boundaries is that the many jurisdictions are all possible funding sources. Some regional initiatives rely on membership dues from participating jurisdictions and stakeholders as part of their funding portfolio. Others earn fees for providing services, such as technical expertise and facilitation or mediation skills.

The longer a regional initiative continues to operate, the more important administrative capacity becomes. Short-lived efforts may do fine operating out of someone's home, but more permanent initiatives need a publicly accessible office and Web site where people can find the organization. Having a presence in a region is as basic and essential as making sure someone is available to answer the phone during business hours.

Shoring up administrative capacity also means maintaining a systematic network of participants through the development and use of phone and email trees and mailing lists. Staff should include information managers (to write and edit publications, develop and maintain a Web site, and interact with the media) and financial managers (to develop and manage a budget, payroll, and a business plan). Most sustainable organizations also rely heavily on administrative assistants to plan and staff meetings and handle the day-to-day logistics of running a collaborative effort. These details may seem mundane and are often overlooked, but it is nearly impossible to sustain a functional organization with a weak administrative infrastructure.

Clear operating protocols are needed as the effort coalesces into something more permanent and questions (and possibly conflicts) arise about roles and responsibilities. It is best to anticipate as many of these issues as possible by drafting protocols that spell out the organizational structure, how decisions are made and by whom, how funding is allocated, and how programs and projects are managed.

Most long-running initiatives have a board of directors, steering committee, or similar guiding panel of leaders. Daily operations are overseen by an executive director or president and staff assigned to specific program areas. An organizational chart can help show the hierarchy and decision-making chain. Also, more than just an accounting of revenues and expenses, a budget is an indicator of priorities and responsibilities among projects and programs.

For the sake of transparency and to build trust and ownership, most regional initiatives make operating protocols and other such information freely available, even showcasing them on a Web site and in published materials. Such transparency makes sense, given that the operating protocols are usually developed by the participants themselves. If the initiative grows more formal, however, these may become codified in statute at a regional, state, or even federal level. Similarly, operating protocols may be shaped in part by other external forces, such as Internal Revenue Service requirements for 501(c)(3) nonprofit status. Again, to remain sustainable, such changes are best driven and guided as much as possible by the participants themselves.

CONCLUSION

Evaluating the progress of regional efforts is a key ingredient for success in working across boundaries. It is the very basis for learning as you go and adapting tools and strategies to better achieve the desired outcomes. The evaluation scorecard and other assessment tools presented here can be tailored to suit the unique circumstances and interests of any region.

In fact, evaluation tools themselves should be evaluated and adapted as they are used so that they, too, can be improved and provide more accurate, helpful feedback. Many regional initiatives routinely use several evaluation strategies at any one time. This allows practitioners to double check and verify the results, and it also sheds light on any problems and successes from more than one angle.

Any regional collaborative effort is only as sustainable as the people involved want it to be. Yet that desire alone may not be enough to support ongoing work. In 20 years of talking with regional practitioners across the country, we have heard time and again that sustained funding is the critical factor in keeping such an effort alive. A supply-side view would say that competition for funding is fierce, and there are never enough dollars to go around. But a demand-side perspective—one that sees regional collaboration as the best response and an essential component for progress—sheds a more helpful light on how regional initiatives can be proactive in supporting and sustaining themselves.

First, carry through with monitoring and evaluation; compare progress against baseline conditions; document success and analyze mistakes;

identify unmet needs and ongoing challenges and opportunities; and brain-storm adaptations to old strategies and invent new ones.

Second, celebrate effectiveness and success; publicize progress; distribute "good news" press releases; post photographs on your Web site; and throw a public party. Make the success personal—get direct quotes from the people who benefited most; thank donors personally for their money; and offer some tangible appreciation to volunteers for their time. Talk to the media and explain how the regional initiative has changed people's lives for the better.

Third, be strategic in riding any swell of enthusiasm and support; trust your action plan; stay true to your compass bearing; and avoid distractions and high-maintenance offers that promise a low return. In short, stay focused and persevere.

Chapter 8

MODELS OF REGIONAL GOVERNANCE

Regional initiatives come in a wide variety of shapes—from informal networks to more formal partnerships to new institutions. Despite their varied forms, however, few regional initiatives are actually designed to govern on land use, natural resource, and environmental issues. To date, most regional initiatives are optional or voluntary—they cannot require compliance, and they have no legal decision-making or implementation authority. At most, they may be advisory, hoping to influence the actions of government. Indeed, there are only a few regional efforts that engage in full-fledged regional governance.

Regional governance models range from voluntary, nonbinding arrangements to strict compliance models, each with its own relative strengths and weaknesses. When people explore creating a formal regional governance structure, they typically make three assumptions. First, a regional land use or water plan or policy is accepted as a good idea. In other words, the region has moved beyond networks and partnerships and is seeking to create a more formal system to govern regional land use. Second, the overarching goal is to pursue a regional vision while respecting the identity and autonomy of local jurisdictions. (As explained later in this chapter, some regions choose to elevate the importance of the region above local jurisdictions—the most extreme case being models that consolidate multiple jurisdictions into one.) And third, effective regional governance requires the sharing of power and resources.

Given these assumptions, the design of a regional governance system revolves around five key questions, which also provide a useful framework for evaluating the strengths and weaknesses of the various models for regional governance.

1. Who develops the regional plan or planning framework?

2. What is the authority of the regional plan?

3. Who participates in the regional governing body?

4. How are decisions made within the regional body?

5. How are disputes resolved between regional and local interests?

FOUR MODELS OF REGIONAL GOVERNANCE

Four models best capture—while also emphasizing the most relevant distinctions of—the range of regional governance as it is currently practiced in the land use context. We describe each model (moving from easiest to sustain to most difficult), illustrate each with one or more case examples, and examine their strengths and weaknesses.

VOLUNTARY, NONBINDING MODELS ■ The easiest approach to regional governance is a voluntary, nonbinding arrangement. The essence of this approach is that participation is voluntary and is often induced by providing incentives such as funding for infrastructure and technical assistance. Where a regional plan is voluntary and nonbinding, decision making tends to be consensus-based and there is rarely any need for a dispute-resolution mechanism. If a particular jurisdiction disagrees with some aspect of a regional plan or vision, it would presumably not participate. In sum, this is a very soft approach to governance and perhaps almost stretches the meaning of governance beyond our definition. Nevertheless, this approach may be the most appropriate given the political culture of a particular region.

Southern California Compass Blueprint. The southern California region is the second largest metropolis in the nation. With a vibrant economy, the region is also one of the most congested, suffers from serious air pollution, and is facing a housing crisis. By the year 2030, another 5 million residents will be added to the existing 18 million, creating more pressure on already congested roadways and scarce housing and threatening advancements the region has already made in air quality.

In 2000, the Southern California Association of Governments (SCAG) initiated the Southern California Compass Blueprint planning process.

SCAG is the largest regional planning agency in the United States, covering an area of more than 38,000 square miles and functioning as the metropolitan planning organization (MPO) for six counties: Imperial, Los Angeles, Orange, San Bernardino, Riverside, and Ventura. SCAG's 76-member governing board, made up of elected officials from all the local governments of the region, makes and implements policy.

To initiate the development of the Compass Blueprint, the governing board created a growth-visioning subcommittee, charging it to develop a plan that promotes livability, mobility, prosperity, and sustainability. The Compass Blueprint process included a technical analysis of growth options and incorporated diverse social values that emerged from extensive public participation.

The Compass Blueprint, adopted in 2004, is notable for its voluntary, incentive-based approach to implementation. SCAG periodically solicits proposals for demonstration projects that exemplify the goals articulated by the Compass Blueprint while creating unique visions of local communities. Cities selected for demonstration projects receive, free of charge, consultant services, technical assistance, and staff time to promote examples of creative, forward-thinking, and sustainable development solutions that fit local needs and support shared regional values.

Envision Utah. Anticipating that the Greater Wasatch area, anchored by Salt Lake City, was expected to add a million more residents by the year 2020, the Envision Utah Public/Private Partnership was formed in January 1997 to develop a quality growth strategy—a vision to protect the region's environment, economic strength, and quality of life. This regional planning process is completely voluntary. No official governmental body—or anyone else for that matter—told civic, business, and other leaders to develop this regional vision and plan.

The reasoning behind the Envision Utah process was to build widespread support from the beginning among citizens, decision makers, and officials who make and implement land use decisions. By building broad-based, grassroots support throughout the process, successful—and voluntary—implementation would be ensured. Such support was generated by convening 135 public meetings attended by more than 4,500 participants; distributing 930,000 questionnaires across the region, to which approximately 23,500 residents responded; and dedicating more than 70,000 hours to technical modeling. In addition, scores of meetings were held with Envision Utah Partners, the steering committee, and local and state officials.

To implement the goals and strategies outlined in the quality growth strategy, Envision Utah provides training and resources to local and state government and private sector planners. Participants continue to educate decision makers and share the goals outlined in the strategy, working closely with local governments to manage growth based on community input. Civic and political support remains strong, and planners throughout the region have embraced the strategy. Envision Utah is one of the most often cited success stories in regional land use planning and has been credited with helping to shape several walkable planned communities and to build support for a light rail system in the region (MacGillis 2006).

Strengths and Weaknesses. The strengths of a voluntary, nonbinding approach to regional governance are that it is very adaptable to local needs and interests and does not rely on formal governmental actions to initiate the process and develop the regional plan or policy. It does, of course, rely on government officials to implement the regional vision. It also provides an excellent place to start when regions are polarized or there is no compelling catalyst around which to mobilize and organize people.

The primary limitations of this model are that it produces regional visions and plans that have no formal teeth—they do not bind local jurisdictions to regional goals and aspirations. Instead, this model relies on regional leaders and champions as well as incentives to persuade local jurisdictions and others to implement the regional plan.

VOLUNTARY, BINDING MODELS ■ In the second approach to regional governance, participation is voluntary but binding once a local jurisdiction opts in. Local jurisdictions are not mandated to implement regional goals and aspirations. Rather, they choose to do so because of incentives, which typically come in the form of funding for infrastructure or technical assistance for planning and development. The authority of a regional plan or policy is thus contingent upon local jurisdictions agreeing to participate and follow through with implementation.

Denver's Mile High Compact. The Mile High Compact is a negotiated agreement among 44 jurisdictions in the Denver metropolitan area that have voluntarily opted in to the program. In addition to moral persuasion and peer pressure, the incentive to join is to improve access to federal transportation dollars. As the regional MPO, the Denver Regional Council of Governments (DRCOG) has significant influence on how federal transportation dollars are spent and has used that role to prioritize funds for regionally significant projects through its Transportation Improvement Program. The program, which cycles every two years, scores projects—whether submitted by an individual jurisdiction or from state or regional transportation bodies—on how well they conform to the regional transportation, growth, and land use policies.

The first notable feature of this model is that once local jurisdictions have signed the compact, they make a commitment to adopt a comprehensive land use plan that includes a common set of elements and to link their comprehensive plans to Metro Vision 2020, the regional growth management plan. They also agree to use growth management tools such as zoning regulations, urban growth boundaries, and development codes, and to work together to guide growth and ensure consistency across local jurisdictions and among local and regional plans.

The implementation of the Mile High Compact is overseen by DRCOG, a nonprofit, voluntary association of 52 local governments. DRCOG is a public agency, but it is not a unit of government. It has no statutory authority to require local governments to be members or to follow its regional plans. DRCOG also cannot tax, issue bonds, or legislate. Each of the local jurisdictions that have signed the Mile High Compact has a vote on DRCOG's board of directors, which makes decisions on the basis of simple majority. The City and County of Denver, as one entity, has two votes and pays dues accordingly.

Although it has never been used, there is also the additional option of an "on demand" weighted vote of the jurisdictions by population (invoking a double-double majority). This weighted vote, in proportion to the population of each jurisdiction, occurs upon specific request by a member and the passage of a resolution by the board of directors (Dempsey, Goetz, and Larson 2000). The DRCOG board also created a plan-consistency checklist so local planning departments can compare their policies with those of

Metro Vision. After completing the checklist, local jurisdictions submit it to DRCOG to certify that their plans are consistent.

The second notable feature of the Mile High Compact flips this idea around—local governments can also propose changes to Metro Vision to improve its consistency with local plans. In other words, the compact acknowledges that changes, goals, and aspirations at the local level should be allowed to inform and influence the shape of the regional plan.

The disputes that emerge while implementing the Mile High Compact tend to focus on the allocation of federal transportation dollars and whose local plan is more consistent with Metro Vision. To resolve disputes, the DRCOG board defers the disagreements back to the disputants and asks them to resolve the issues before either one can be considered for funding. DRCOG provides facilitation and mediation support when and where necessary. Although compliance with the Mile High Compact is voluntary, the regional goals and aspirations have effectively been institutionalized as the norm.

Chicago 2040 Regional Framework. The governance structure of this ambitious regional plan relies on a carefully articulated set of expectations for regional and local actors. Rather than prescribe solutions, the 2040 Regional Framework guides the integration of regional and local plans, policies, and goals. As the primary convener, the Northeastern Illinois Planning Commission (NIPC) continues to help implement the 2040 plan by facilitating meetings, providing technology tools, and conducting statistical forecasts and other research while coordinating agencies and local governments. NIPC also will develop a report card of performance indicators aligned with the plan's five core themes. Published annually, this tool will help establish accountability for implementation progress, growth, development, and redevelopment.

Decisions are made by a 15-member board of directors. The mayor of Chicago appoints five members; the Cook County board president appoints one directly and appoints four others in cooperation with the mayors from each of four sections of Cook County; and mayors and chief elected county officials from the collar counties appoint five members cooperatively. Concurrence of four-fifths of the board members in office is needed for any board action.

This regional governance framework is notable for two reasons. First, it acknowledges the importance of thinking like a region, yet asserts that land use and conservation work are primarily in the hands of local governments. Second, like the Mile High Compact, the 2040 Regional Framework provides funding for infrastructure (mostly transportation) as an incentive for local jurisdictions to buy into the goals and aspirations of the regional plan. The framework informs the regional transportation plan, which guides transportation planning and investment in the region. Initiatives within local jurisdictions must be consistent with the regional framework if they want to receive federal funding.

Strengths and Weaknesses. Voluntary, binding models of regional governance have two primary advantages. First, local jurisdictions choose whether or not to participate—it is not mandatory or top-down. Second, if a local jurisdiction opts in (because of the incentives or peer pressure), then it must pursue the goals and aspirations of the regional plan or policy. In many ways, this provides the best of two worlds and allows a region to build a positive, constructive culture of regional thinking and action. The downside with this model is that it has little to no enforcement authority over nonparticipating jurisdictions. As such, inconsistent and/or incompatible land uses may occur when adjacent jurisdictions are operating according to different goals and standards.

STRICT COMPLIANCE MODELS ■ The essence of this third approach is that local jurisdictions must comply with regional goals as articulated through some type of formal, public process—most often legislation. In this respect, the regional plan is binding on local jurisdictions. Participation is mandatory, decisions are typically made on the basis of a simple majority, and disputes are resolved through formal mechanisms, such as mediation, arbitration, and deference to an independent third party.

Minneapolis and St. Paul Metropolitan Council. The Minnesota legislature created the Met Council in 1967 to develop and implement a regional plan focused on transportation, aviation, wastewater treatment, and parks and open space. The council consists of 17 members: 16 represent a geographic district in the seven-county area and the chairperson serves at large. All members are appointed by the governor and confirmed by the Minnesota Senate. Decisions within the council are made by simple majority.

Perhaps the most notable feature of this model is that local communities within the affected region are required to adopt comprehensive plans that are consistent with the council's regional plan. The council guides capital investments, which are supplemented by federally mandated integrated planning for wastewater/stormwater and transportation/air quality. Local communities must comply with the regional plan. In return, they receive technical assistance through forecasts, a local planning handbook, and comprehensive plan reviews. Incentive programs provide grants to expand housing choices, promote connected development, and clean up contaminated land for redevelopment.

The statute creating the Met Council lays out a process for resolving disputes, such as those that might arise when a community fears it will be negatively affected by a proposed action in a neighboring community. In the event of such disputes, the Met Council forms a significance review committee to evaluate the proposed project and determine whether it will substantially impact service levels of major transportation facilities, local or regional sewer and stormwater plans, open space and recreational resources, and other environmental considerations. The committee may defer the determination to a mediator or administrative law judge. The primary criterion for a "substantial impact" is the degree to which a proposal is consistent with or conforms to the regional plan. The outcome of the assessment may require the developer to modify the proposal to make it consistent with existing policies and plans; it may require amendments to local or regional plans to accommodate the proposed development; or suspension of the proposal for one year may be required.

Portland Metro Council. In 1992, citizens in the Portland, Oregon, region created a similar regional governance system that is authorized to develop and enforce implementation of a regional land use plan. Metro's plans and programs are focused on urban revitalization, transit-oriented development, housing choice and affordability, new (greenfield) development, brownfield redevelopment, and nature-friendly development.

The Oregon legislature has granted Metro several specific land use planning powers including: (1) coordinating between regional and local comprehensive plans in adopting a regional urban growth boundary; (2) requiring

consistency of local comprehensive plans with statewide and regional planning goals; and (3) planning for activities of metropolitan significance including, but not limited to, transportation, water quality, air quality, and solid
waste. City and county comprehensive plans and land use regulations must
comply with the regional plan within two years of its adoption. To ensure
compliance, the local land use plans are reviewed by the state land conservation and development commission. If there are disagreements, Metro adjudi-
cates and determines the consistency of local plans.

The most notable feature of this model is that participants on the
Portland Metro Council are elected. The president is elected in a regionwide
vote, while six other councilors are elected in nonpartisan races by district
every four years. One of the limitations of this process is that it potentially
creates tension, if not conflict, among other elected officials.

Another example, the Ada County Highway District in Idaho, is an
elected regional body that provides transportation planning and maintenance for the county and six cities. In theory, it makes sense to have one
consolidated highway district serve multiple jurisdictions, but conflict still
arises over the question of which elected officials set what priorities.

Growth Plan for the Greater Golden Horseshoe in Toronto. The strict compliance model used in Toronto, Ontario, is notable for two reasons. First,
the minister of Public Infrastructure Renewal develops the regional growth
plan—unlike in other models, where the regional governing body itself
creates the regional plan. Participation by local jurisdictions is mandatory;
they must bring their official plans into conformity with the growth plan
within three years.

The second reason concerns how it resolves discrepancies between local
jurisdictions and the regional plan. If, in the minister's opinion, a local plan
does not conform to the growth plan or is not brought into conformity with
the growth plan within three years, the minister may request a change to the
official plan to resolve nonconformity. Jointly with the minister of Municipal Affairs and Housing, the minister of Public Infrastructure Renewal may
amend an official plan to resolve nonconformity. However, if a local municipal plan or bylaw conflicts with the regional plan, the regional plan prevails.

Strengths and Weaknesses. The strengths of the strict compliance model
are obvious. Regional plans have teeth because they are established by an

official act of government; local jurisdictions must conform to regional goals, thereby providing regional consistency and efficiency; and typically more resources (staff, expertise, and funding) are available than in the voluntary models of regional governance.

The limitations of this model are also somewhat obvious—regional commitments are imposed on local jurisdictions, whether they like it or not. This dynamic may erode the sense of local identity and autonomy and may also stifle innovation if local ideas and actions are not consistent with regional goals and aspirations. Finally, regional governments, like other large organizations, may become inflexible and bureaucratic.

Perhaps the most challenging policy—and political—question within this model of strict compliance is how to resolve disputes when local needs and interests conflict with the regional vision. Responses to this question range from asserting the primacy of the regional plan to deferring the dispute to an independent third party.

One approach to resolving disputes, more common in Canada than in the United States, is to create an elaborate system of representation and voting mechanisms. Such systems may be based on the notion of a double majority in which decisions must be approved by a majority of the region's municipalities, which in turn collectively represent a majority of the region's population (Minister's Council on Municipal Sustainability 2007).

In British Columbia, for example, regional districts rely on creative voting schemes that seek to balance representation by population and representation by jurisdiction, as follows. A voting unit is established for each regional district, such as one vote per one thousand population. The voting unit is usually set to match the size of the smallest municipality. The number of votes a municipality or electoral area is entitled to is then determined by dividing the population of the political unit by the voting unit with the result raised to the next whole number. Finally, the number of directors for each political unit is determined by dividing the number of votes by the number five. This procedure ensures that each political unit has at least one director, while giving larger jurisdictions more than one director and more votes.

The legislation that created this system provides for two different kinds of votes within a regional district. Corporate votes, in which all board directors are entitled to vote on the basis of one director, one vote, are used to make decisions on any issue that requires the input and deliberation of the entire body, such as establishing a new service, contracting for a debt, or adopting the annual budget and dealing with matters of corporate procedure or staffing. Stakeholder votes, by contrast, allow only directors participating in a regional service to vote in accordance with the principle of representation by population. This effectively means that votes are weighted to the population rather than to jurisdictional boundaries and that more populous jurisdictions will have more votes than less populous jurisdictions.

Within the context of both voting systems, there is a very strong presumption and culture that district boards will seek consensus. From a practical perspective, then, the voting systems are largely designed to specify who participates in a particular consensus-building process, rather than enforcing a particular voting scheme per se.

Another notable feature of this strict compliance model is that all affected municipalities must approve the regional growth strategy developed by the district board. This dynamic suggests that, at least in theory, there is some give and take between regional and local interests. Once the regional growth strategy is approved by all jurisdictions, all bylaws, plans, and services undertaken by a regional district must be consistent with the regional growth strategy. Individual jurisdictional or community plans must include a regional context statement that explains how the community plans are consistent with the regional growth strategy. These statements must be approved by the regional district board and updated at least once every five years. If a dispute emerges between a local jurisdiction or community and the regional district, the Ministry of Community Service provides a range of dispute resolution services.

CONSOLIDATION MODELS ■ The fourth model—and typically the most difficult to implement—is consolidation of multiple, independent local jurisdictions into one regional governing body.

Unigov: Indianapolis and Marion County, Indiana. In the late 1960s, community leaders in Indianapolis and Marion County began looking for ways to reduce the costs and inefficiencies of operating separate city and county governments. Richard Lugar, then mayor of Indianapolis and now a U.S. senator, also saw a unified government as a way to create a forum for an "honest and open discussion of racial issues, of social justice, and of how we could employ all our creative and financial talents to build a city that could provide public safety, better job opportunities, stronger cultural institutions, and a potential tax base to pay for these ambitions" (Lugar 2005). A plan was developed to consolidate city and county governments, but some satellite communities pushed back out of distrust and fear of losing local control. In the end, it took special legislation at the state level to approve the plan, creating Unigov and expanding the city's boundaries to include all of Marion County.

The legislation greatly increased the city's tax base and gave Unigov powers and functions previously parceled out among many agencies and departments in both the city and county governments. Under Unigov, a 29-member city-county council levies taxes, adopts budgets, and enacts ordinances. Twenty-five of the members are elected by the voters in their districts and four at-large members are elected by the voters of the entire county. The mayor is chief executive officer of both the city and county, overseeing five departments: capital asset management, metropolitan development, public works, public safety, and parks and recreation.

Not all functions of local government were absorbed by Unigov, however. School districts and fire departments remain independent. Also, the cities of Beech Grove, Lawrence, Southport, and the town of Speedway, all within Marion County, retained their autonomy. Residents of these communities wanted to be excluded from the consolidation. They continue to pay county taxes, but they elect their own local mayors, councils, and boards. Because decisions made in Indianapolis affect all of Marion County, residents of these excluded towns are still eligible to vote in Indianapolis mayoral elections and are represented in the city-county council by their district member and the four at-large council members.

Further legislation passed by the Indiana general assembly in 2005 allowed for the consolidation of city and county budget and human resources functions and the merger of the county sheriff and the Indianapolis city police departments. Local government staffing and functions were streamlined, with some functions eliminated at the local level and assigned to existing county-level offices. The mayor's office projected that these more recent consolidation measures would further improve public services and efficiencies and save city-county taxpayers an estimated $35 million each year (Peterson 2005).

After nearly four decades of consolidated government, Indianapolis is a thriving city, the twelfth largest by population in the United States. Yet Unigov still struggles with budget shortfalls and inefficiencies of scale in the delivery of certain services. The region's fire departments, for instance, remain localized, meaning that it takes 10 fire chiefs to oversee the same territory as a single chief of police. Overall, Lugar and others say that consolidation ushered in a more cost-effective, progressive era for the Indianapolis region (Lugar 2005).

Other Examples. Unigov has served as a model for consolidation in other metropolitan areas (including Nashville, Tennessee, and on a limited basis for public health care, Toledo, Ohio), but even its proponents warn that it is not a panacea. "I wouldn't Xerox the Unigov model," says Indiana Governor Mitch Daniels, "but [Indianapolis] is generally considered one of the most successful cities in America, let alone Indiana" (Howey 2008).

Consolidation is not always driven by the desire to improve service delivery, capture economies of scale, or better coordinate land use and transportation planning. In November 2000, voters in Louisville and Jefferson County, Kentucky, approved a proposal to merge city and county governments (K. Foster 2001). This merger was about political stature. By consolidating the two independent jurisdictions into Greater Louisville, the region climbed overnight from sixty-fifth largest in the nation (based on population) to twenty-third. The merger dispelled the sense of "obscurity and the humiliation of being Kentucky's 'second city' to Lexington and a poor cousin to rivals Nashville and Indianapolis, each of which gained political brawn through city-county consolidations over thirty years ago" (K. Foster 2001, 31).

Auckland, New Zealand, is attempting to create a "supercity" by consolidating four cities, eight councils, and the existing Auckland Regional Council (One Auckland Trust 2008). While many of the affected jurisdictions apparently agree that regional governance needs to be improved, particularly in managing growth and development, recent news stories variously conclude: "This is one of the most barefaced bids for power by the few over the many" (Bradford 2006); "[I]t (is) totally undemocratic and it undermines the whole idea of democracy" (Gay 2008); and it will not happen without a "willingness from all parties involved to cede a greater degree of autonomy" in the interests of regional goals (Gay 2008).

Strengths and Weaknesses. These examples bring us back to the fundamental principle behind regional governance: regardless of which model is used, effective regional governance requires the sharing of power and resources. The primary argument in support of the consolidation model is that a single, regional governing body can deliver services more efficiently, equalize taxes, effectively resolve place-based disputes among previously independent jurisdictions, and streamline decision making. The primary argument against consolidation is that it weakens or even eliminates local identity and sense of community. It may also erode relationships and hamper implementation of regional goals if consolidation is imposed on recalcitrant local jurisdictions.

CONCLUSION

Regional governance is neither necessary nor desirable in all regions. When and where it does make sense, regions may choose from a menu of models or create hybrids tailored to their needs and interests. Among regional initiatives at the beginning of the twenty-first century, the general trend is to answer the five key questions we posed at the outset of this chapter in accordance with the following guidelines.

The first question—Who develops the regional plan?—is foundational because it speaks directly to the issues of ownership, buy-in, and willingness and capacity to implement the plan. The options here are: (1) an ad hoc association of people from the public, private, and nonprofit sectors; (2) elected officials, planners, or both from the affected jurisdictions; (3) a regional governing body created either by the affected jurisdictions or some higher level of government; and (4) a higher level of government, such as a state or province. Using widely accepted criteria from multiparty negotiation theory (satisfaction of outcomes, stability of outcomes, transaction costs, and impact on relationships) the best approach here is to allow and encourage the affected jurisdictions to help shape and revise the plan as needed.

The second question—What is the authority of the plan?—focuses on whether a regional plan is simply advisory, or if it requires the affected local jurisdictions to implement the goals and standards articulated in the regional plan. As explained above, the options here range from voluntary, nonbinding plans to voluntary, binding plans to strict compliance. Another typology is advisory, mandatory, or contingent, where access to specific services, such as funding or technical services, is contingent on implementing regional goals and aspirations. Given that most people and institutions do not like to be told what to do, the best approach here is to create the right set of incentives so that local jurisdictions will choose to comply with the regional vision.

The third question—Who participates in the regional governing body?—is complicated by a series of related questions. Which existing local jurisdictions should be included in the regional system of governance? (The answer to this question may vary depending on whether the system is designed to be comprehensive and inclusive or adaptive to particular issues [e.g., transportation corridors, open space corridors, watersheds, air quality].) Is participation voluntary or mandatory? How many representatives should each participating jurisdiction have at the table? Should this be based on population or some other variable such as level of government or type of municipality (i.e., urban, suburban, or rural)? And how do the representatives get to the table—are they self-selected, appointed by some executive official (e.g., a governor or premier), or elected?

The theory and practice of multiparty negotiation and conflict resolution strongly suggest that the best approach here is to allow participating jurisdictions to select their own representatives. The rationale is that they will have more confidence in both the process and outcomes if their interests are represented by a person of their own choosing.

The fourth question—How does a regional body make decisions?—includes options such as consensus (defined as unanimous agreement), simple majority, super majority, and various voting schemes (including but not limited to double majority and/or weighted vote). Once again, practical experience suggests that the best approach here is to seek consensus, but provide a fall-back decision rule.

One essential consideration is that such issues as who participates, how many representatives are included per jurisdiction, and so on, become more critical to resolve if a regional body is making decisions on the basis of consensus. If the decision rule is to seek consensus, the smartest strategy is to send the best negotiator to the table. On the other hand, if a regional body is making decisions on the basis of some type of voting scheme, the only thing that matters is how many representatives a particular jurisdiction has at the table. Moreover, the use of a voting scheme may compel participants to modify their negotiating tactics from those suitable in a consensus approach to those suited for a coalition-building approach.

The fifth question—How are disputes resolved between regional and local interests?—presumes that local jurisdictions are required to implement the vision, principles, or standards articulated in a regional plan, otherwise there would be no dispute. The options here revolve around tabling the discussion pending further review (and providing additional information and education), negotiation, mediation, arbitration (binding or not), voting (including weighted voting schemes), and deferring the dispute to an independent third party (such as a higher level of government or the courts). Another option is simply to assert as a matter of policy that the regional vision takes priority over local needs and interests. A corollary to this policy is to allow local jurisdictions to propose changes to the regional plan to balance local and regional needs and interests. The best approach here is for the affected jurisdictions to maintain as much control over the decision-making or dispute-resolution process as possible, rather than deferring the resolution to an independent third party.

While these questions and guidelines provide a useful place to start, there is little empirical evidence to support one model of regional governance as being superior to another. The evaluation tools presented in chapter 7 could be used to weigh the advantages and disadvantages of these various models.

Although there is a significant body of experience on regional governance related to land use and conservation in North America, much of that experience—and the literature examining it—has focused on metropolitan areas. Experiments with regional governance in rural areas are also rare, especially when it comes to public lands, mixed-ownership landscapes, and ecosystems. As citizens, decision makers, and advocates continue to experiment with alternative approaches to regional governance in all these contexts, it would be wise to take a hard look at the lessons learned from regional governance in the water resources community and habitat conservation planning. Given that most watersheds cut across multiple local, state, national, and even international boundaries, it is not surprising that there has been a long history of experiments in how to share and govern this vital resource. Eventually, consistent with John Wesley Powell's vision of watershed commonwealths, we may arrive at the point where we govern land, water, and the built environment on the basis of common regions.

Chapter 9

IMPROVING REGIONAL COLLABORATION

Working across boundaries—regional collaboration—is emerging as an essential component of land use, natural resource, and environmental policy making in the twenty-first century. Whether the issues involve rapid growth and its consequences, the need to diversify and expand the economic base, or the desire to conserve landscapes, the best solutions are often found by working across the boundaries created by governmental jurisdictions, economies, values, and professional disciplines. Indeed, in many cases this is the only way to resolve such issues effectively.

Regional collaboration resists being pigeonholed. In fact, the range of formal and informal experiments in regional collaboration in North America today aptly demonstrates that there is no single model to close the gap in governance caused by transboundary issues. Innovative responses are emerging at all levels and among all sectors—public, private, and nongovernmental organizations. This diversity of approaches and strategies is a rich source of inspiration, experience-based insights, and potential best practices for anyone considering engaging in regional collaboration. Regional practitioners continue to refine the theory and practice of working across boundaries, and their efforts suggest that future success can be enhanced through the following actions.

1. RECOGNIZE THAT REGIONAL COLLABORATION IS BOTH A PROCESS AND A GOAL ■ This book focuses largely on the process of regional collaboration—how to build bridges among people who care about regional issues. We have not prescribed specific solutions or illustrated preferred outcomes. In this respect, regional collaboration is one of many experiments in democracy and governance. However, regional collaboration is not an end in itself. People who engage in regional collaboration are committed to people, place, and prosperity.

While the objectives of individual regional initiatives vary, most participants seem to be keenly interested in promoting and sustaining livable
communities, vibrant economies, and healthy environments.

**2. INCREASE THE UNDERSTANDING AND SKILLS OF PEOPLE
INVOLVED** ■ Most regional practitioners learn on the job. As such,
there is a growing need for workshops, seminars, and conferences where
participants and scholars can share stories and learn from each other.
Several regions host their own leadership institutes, increasing the corps
of homegrown leaders schooled in collaborative problem solving. The
Alliance for Regional Stewardship offers a Learning Network that connects
members for peer-to-peer assistance. The alliance also convenes annual
forums for practitioners to exchange ideas and develop and refine skills.

The Lincoln Institute of Land Policy offers an interactive Web site that
provides best practices and examples and allows regional practitioners to
share the lessons learned from their own regional experience. The Lincoln
Institute also sponsors place-based projects on innovative approaches to
regional collaboration and offers an applied short course on regional collaboration. The demand for education and training opportunities seems to
be increasing as regional practitioners seek to develop and refine their skills
and build the capacity of their regions.

3. BUILD A CONSTITUENCY FOR REGIONAL COLLABORATION ■
In addition to supporting regional practitioners, there is also a need to raise
awareness, understanding, and interest among other people in the public,
private, and nonprofit sectors. A focus on communications planning can
help practitioners target different audiences and appropriately tailor the
message of regional collaboration. Emphasizing success stories as well as
the critical roles of different actors can inspire and motivate people to think
about the need for and value of working across boundaries.

It makes sense to build on existing organizational infrastructures,
such as the National Association of Regional Councils and the Renewable
Natural Resources Foundation (a coalition of natural resource professionals
representing all disciplines and sectors). It is also important to reach out
to associations of governors, legislators, city and county officials, and the
myriad groups interested in and affected by land use, natural resources, and
environmental issues.

4. PREPARE TOMORROW'S LEADERS ■ One of the best ways to build
a constituency for regional collaboration is to instill such a worldview in
tomorrow's leaders. Traditional programs and courses in regional planning
provide a valuable infrastructure on which to build. But many of these
programs need to move beyond the conventional model of planning to
integrate coalition-building models such as those presented in this book.

Emerging programs in bioregional planning at Utah State University, ecosystem management at the University of Michigan, and natural
resources conflict resolution at the University of Montana provide more
focused and refined sets of theories and practical strategies for regional
collaboration. It would be helpful to conduct a more complete survey of
these innovative programs and to convene a group of program directors to
compare notes, highlight curriculum content, and identify additional ways
to prepare tomorrow's leaders.

**5. CREATE LEGAL AND INSTITUTIONAL INCENTIVES TO FOSTER AND
SUPPORT REGIONAL COLLABORATION** ■ Working across boundaries
can be improved by creating the legal and institutional structures to allow
(at least experimentally) or outright encourage and support regional
collaboration. To begin, a better understanding is needed of what types of
institutional arrangements are necessary to support regional collaboration.
In some cases, legislators should carve out some legal space to allow public
officials and others to experiment with alternative models of governance,
particularly when the issues involve federal lands and resources (McKinney
and Harmon 2004). Based on recommendations from the White House
Conference on Cooperative Conservation (2005), several federal land
management agencies are working toward making collaboration, including
regional collaboration, part of performance evaluations and career
advancement. Dodge (1996) offers a robust menu of other strategies
to create the right set of legal and institutional incentives for regional
collaboration.

**6. ENCOURAGE PHILANTHROPIC FOUNDATIONS TO INVEST IN
REGIONAL COLLABORATION** ■ Grant makers also must play a critical
role in promoting and supporting experiments in regional collaboration.
Too often no other institution can support these kinds of innovations.
Governments are fiscally constrained and often threatened by changes

to the system of governance, while the business community does not always see the immediate payoff from such experiments. Philanthropic foundations can play a critical role in helping design and test new models for working across boundaries and in disseminating lessons learned.

7. DEVELOP AND REFINE THE PRESCRIPTIVE FRAMEWORK FOR REGIONAL COLLABORATION ■ The principles of regional collaboration presented in this book, along with the practical strategies and theoretical literature presented on the Lincoln Institute of Land Policy's Web site, represent a beginning. Much can still be done to improve our understanding of the most effective theories and practices for regional collaboration. We see a need for further research to identify and describe problems associated with regional collaboration; explain the causes of those problems; propose solutions and articulate the reasons why they should work; and implement the proposed solutions (MacArthur Foundation 2007).

This research agenda should be linked to regional practitioners through a variety of media including conferences, journals, editorials, and the Internet, thereby creating an ongoing network for learning, adapting, and improving the practice of regional collaboration. In addition to tackling specific problems, one possible future direction for research on regional collaboration is a national innovation assessment that collects, analyzes, and reports results on an annual basis. This could be done in cooperation with national organizations that are already working in this field, such as the Lincoln Institute, the Alliance for Regional Stewardship, the National Association of Regional Councils, and others.

8. EXPAND THE PRACTICE OF REGIONAL COLLABORATION ■ The overwhelming body of practical experience with regional collaboration has focused on metropolitan areas and river basins. While there is a compelling need for regional collaboration in these contexts, we should also explore how the principles and strategies of regional collaboration might be applied to megaregions, clarify the interplay between megaregions defined by population and their corresponding ecological regions, and adapt learning-support technologies to rural communities undergoing dramatic change as well as to large mixed-ownership landscapes and ecosystems, such as the Crown of the Continent.

Taken together, these actions will move both the theory and practice of regional collaboration forward. Given better access to information and clearer expectations from funders (both public and private), land and resource planners and managers, civic leaders, decision makers, and citizens will be better able to keep up with the pace of change and respond to escalating demands on our landscapes and communities. As more people recognize the cross-cutting nature of many of today's issues and problems, we hope the concepts, tools, and strategies offered here prove to be useful and productive.

Appendix

PARTICIPANT SATISFACTION SCORECARD

Name of Regional Forum _____

1. What primary interest do you represent on behalf of a stakeholder group? (Please check only one)

❑ Ranching/farming　　　　❑ Wildlife/fish　　　　❑ Local gov't
❑ Timber　　　　　　　　　❑ Wilderness　　　　　❑ State gov't
❑ Mining (incl. oil & gas)　❑ Conservation　　　　❑ Federal gov't
❑ Motorized recreation　　　❑ Non-motorized recreation　❑ Tribal gov't
❑ Outfitting/guiding　　　　❑ Hunting　　　　　　　❑ Water-right holders
❑ Utility company　　　　　❑ Tourism industry　　　❑ University/college
❑ Other. Please describe:

2. How long have you participated in this particular forum? (Please check only one)

❑ 3 months or less　　❑ 4 – 12 months　　❑ 1 – 2 years　　❑ 3 years or more

3. Have you participated directly in other regional processes? (Please check only one)

❑ No.　　❑ Yes, 1 – 3 processes.　　❑ Yes, 4 – 6 processes.　　❑ Yes, 7 or more processes.

4. What process would you have used to address this situation if a regional forum weren't available?

❑ No action　　　　　❑ Direct pressure on decision maker(s)　　❑ Litigation
❑ Lobbying　　　　　❑ Proposed legislation　　　　　　　　❑ Citizen initiative
❑ Citizen petition　　❑ Other. Please describe:

5. Compare this regional collaborative process to your next best option (from #4 above). In your opinion, which of the two would most likely:

Cost less?	❑ collaboration	❑ other option
Take less time?	❑ collaboration	❑ other option
Improve communication among participants?	❑ collaboration	❑ other option
Produce a more effective, lasting outcome?	❑ collaboration	❑ other option

6. Would you recommend a regional collaborative process to address similar issues?

❑ Yes.　❑ No. Please explain: _____
_____

7. How could this process be improved? _____
_____

Evaluating Regional Collaboration

For each statement, please check whether you think that aspect of the process is important or unimportant. Also circle the number that best matches your level of agreement with each statement. 1 = completely disagree, 2 = strongly disagree, 3 = disagree, 4 = indifferent, 5 = agree, 6 = strongly agree, 7 = completely agree.

	Important	Unimportant	Circle One
Working Relationships			
The process helped build trust among participants.	❑	❑	1 2 3 4 5 6 7
The process improved communication among participants.	❑	❑	1 2 3 4 5 6 7
I gained insights about others' views and values.	❑	❑	1 2 3 4 5 6 7
I would negotiate other issues with the same participants.	❑	❑	1 2 3 4 5 6 7
The process improved my ability to participate in collaborative forums.	❑	❑	1 2 3 4 5 6 7
Quality of the Process			
Everyone who wanted to participate had a fair chance to do so.	❑	❑	1 2 3 4 5 6 7
Participants' concerns were respected.	❑	❑	1 2 3 4 5 6 7
The process fostered information gathering as a group.	❑	❑	1 2 3 4 5 6 7
Participants had access to the information needed to make good decisions.	❑	❑	1 2 3 4 5 6 7
The process fostered learning as a group.	❑	❑	1 2 3 4 5 6 7
The group considered different options for resolving the issue.	❑	❑	1 2 3 4 5 6 7
Participants kept their constituents informed.	❑	❑	1 2 3 4 5 6 7
Participants effectively represented their constituents at the table.	❑	❑	1 2 3 4 5 6 7
There was a way to address participants' concerns about the process.	❑	❑	1 2 3 4 5 6 7
Gains and losses were fairly distributed among all participants.	❑	❑	1 2 3 4 5 6 7
The process was efficient. It was time well spent.	❑	❑	1 2 3 4 5 6 7
The process was cost effective. It was money well spent.	❑	❑	1 2 3 4 5 6 7
The public was able to review and comment on the process.	❑	❑	1 2 3 4 5 6 7
The Outcome			
An agreement (Recommendations, MOUs etc.) was reached to resolve key issues.	❑	❑	1 2 3 4 5 6 7
The agreement was ratified by everyone needed to implement it.	❑	❑	1 2 3 4 5 6 7
I trust that the agreement will be implemented in good faith.	❑	❑	1 2 3 4 5 6 7
The agreement will be responsive to new information, interests, and ideas.	❑	❑	1 2 3 4 5 6 7
The outcome satisfies my basic interest.	❑	❑	1 2 3 4 5 6 7
The outcome is better than what I could get from another process.	❑	❑	1 2 3 4 5 6 7
The situation surrounding this issue is better than before.	❑	❑	1 2 3 4 5 6 7
The underlying issue was resolved; it will not likely recur.	❑	❑	1 2 3 4 5 6 7
We could not have effectively resolved this issue through any other process.	❑	❑	1 2 3 4 5 6 7

References

Adler, Peter S., and Juliana E. Birkhoff. n.d. *Building trust: When knowledge from "here" meets knowledge from "away."* Portland, OR: National Policy Consensus Center.

Alliance for Regional Stewardship. 2002. *Best practices scan: Regional leadership development initiatives.* Denver, CO: Alliance for Regional Stewardship (February). www.regionalstewardship.org

Al-Qudsi, Sulayman. 2005. *Potential effects of energy megatrends on the city of Calgary: A long term view.* Calgary, AB: City of Calgary. http://sshqudsi.com/downloads/ImagineCalgary.pdf

Atlantic Center for the Environment. 1986. Beyond boundaries: A look at bioregionalism. *Nexus* 8(4): 1–12.

Beatley, Timothy. 1995. Habitat conservation plans: A new tool to resolve land use conflicts. *Land Lines* (September).

Bettison, David G., John K. Kenward, and Larrie Taylor. 1975. *Urban affairs in Alberta.* Edmonton, AB: University of Alberta Press.

Bingham, Gail. 2003. *When the sparks fly: Building consensus when the science is contested.* Washington, DC: Resolve.

Blomgren Bingham, Lisa, Tina Nabatchi, and Rosemary O'Leary. 2005. The new governance: Practices and processes for stakeholder and citizen participation in the work of government. *Public Administration Review* 65(5): 547–558.

Bradford, Sue. 2006. "Aucklund supercity an affront to democracy." Green Party of Aotearoa New Zealand (September 13). www.greens.org.nz/node/16769

Brail, Richard K., ed. 2008. *Planning support systems for cities and regions.* Cambridge, MA: Lincoln Institute of Land Policy.

Brunner, Ronald D., Toddi A. Steelman, Lindy Coe-Juell, Christina M. Cromley, Christine M. Edwards, and Donna W. Tucker. 2005. *Adaptive governance: Integrating science, policy, and decision making.* New York: Columbia University Press.

California Center for Regional Leadership. 2007. *California regional progress report.* California Center for Regional Leadership (November). www.calregions.org/

Calthorpe, Peter, and William Fulton. 2001. *The regional city.* Washington, DC: Island Press.

Campoli, Julie, and Alex S. MacLean. 2007. *Visualizing density.* Cambridge, MA: Lincoln Institute of Land Policy.

Carbonell, Armando, and Robert D. Yaro. 2005. American spatial development and the new megalopolis. *Land Lines* 17(2): 1–4.

Carrier, Amy, and Allan Wallis. 2005. *Regional indicators: Telling stories, measuring trends, inspiring action.* Monograph series 10. Denver, CO: Alliance for Regional Stewardship.

Cartwright, Suzanne D., and Victoria R. Wilbur. 2005. *Translating a regional vision into action.* Washington, DC: Urban Land Institute.

Center for Sustainable Destinations. 2008. www.nationalgeographic.com/travel/sustainable/

CH2MHILL. 2007. *Planning and technical study on water and wastewater servicing in the Calgary region.* Calgary, AB: Calgary Regional Partnership (June).

Clark, Tim W., and Steven C. Minta. 1995. The greater Yellowstone ecosystem: A scientific, managerial, and policy revolution in the making? In *Barriers and bridges for the renewal of regional ecosystems,* eds. C. S. Holling, L. H. Gunderson, and S. S. Light. New York: Columbia University Press.

Coglianese, Cary. 2003. Is satisfaction success? Evaluating public participation and regulatory policymaking. In *The promise and performance of environmental conflict resolution,* eds. R. O'Leary and L. B. Bingham. Washington, DC: Resources for the Future.

Colorado College. n.d. Colorado College State of the Rockies Project. www.coloradocollege.edu/stateoftherockies/

Consensus Building Institute. 1998. How to conduct a conflict assessment. *CBI Reports* (Spring).

Couroux, David, Noel Keough, Byron Miller, and Jesse Row. 2006. *Overcoming barriers to sustainable urban development: Toward smart growth in Calgary.* Calgary, AB: Calgary Citizens' Forum.

Daniels, Steven E., and Gregg B. Walker. 2001. *Working through environmental conflict: The collaborative learning approach.* Westport, CT: Praeger.

Dempsey, Paul Stephen, Andrew Goetz, and Carl Larson. 2000. Metropolitan planning organizations: An assessment of the transportation planning process. A report to Congress. Denver, CO: University of Denver Intermodal Transportation Institute and the National Center for Intermodal Transportation. www.du.edu/transportation/TransportationResearchProjects/MPOStudy.html

Derthcik, Martha. 1974. *Between state and nation: Regional organizations of the United States.* Washington, DC: Brookings Institution.

Dodge, William R. 1996. *Regional excellence: Governing together to compete globally and flourish locally.* Washington, DC: National League of Cities.

Donahue, Michael J. 1987. Alternative institutional arrangements for Great Lakes management: An analysis of generic institutional forms. In *Institutional arrangements for Great Lakes management: Past practices and future alternatives.* Ann Arbor: Michigan Sea Grant College Program.

Ehrmann, John R., and Barbara L. Stinson. 1999. Joint fact-finding and the use of technical experts. In *The consensus building handbook: A comprehensive guide to reaching agreement,* eds. Lawrence Susskind, Sarah McKearnan, and Jennifer Thomas-Larmer. Thousand Oaks, CA: Sage Publications.

Fisher, Roger, and William Ury. 1981. *Getting to yes: Negotiating agreement without giving in.* New York: Penguin Books.

Foster, Charles H. W. 1990. What makes regional organizations succeed or fail? In *International and transboundary water resources issues.* Middleburg, VA: American Water Resources Association.

———. 1997. *Managing resources as whole systems: A primer for managers.* Discussion paper E-97-15. Cambridge, MA: Harvard University, Kennedy School of Government.

Foster, Charles H. W., and William B. Meyer. 2000. *The Harvard environmental regionalism project.* Cambridge, MA: Harvard University, Kennedy School of Government.

Foster, Kathryn A. 2001. *Regionalism on purpose.* Cambridge, MA: Lincoln Institute of Land Policy.

Gastil, John, and Peter Levine, eds. 2005. *The deliberative democracy handbook: Strategies for effective civic engagement in the 21st century.* San Francisco: Jossey-Bass.

Gay, Edward. 2008. Mayors slam supercity proposal as land grab. In *New Zealand Herald* (April 1). www.nzherald.co.nz/local-government/news

Harris, Elizabeth, Chase Huntley, William Mangle, and Naureen Rana. 2001. Transboundary collaboration in ecosystem management: Integrating lessons from experience. Master's thesis. University of Michigan, School of Natural Resources and Environment.

Henton, Doug, John Melville, and John Parr. 2006. *Regional stewardship and collaborative governance: Implementation that produces results.* Monograph series 11. Denver, CO: Alliance for Regional Stewardship. www.regionalstewardship.org

Hope, Marty. 2007. Record setting pace normal. *Calgary Herald* (March 24).

———. 2008. Wheels turning for commuter plan. *Calgary Herald* (August 9).

Hopkins, Lewis D., and Marisa Zapata, eds. 2007. *Engaging the future: Forecasts, scenarios, plans, and projects.* Cambridge, MA: Lincoln Institute of Land Policy.

Howey, Brian A. 2008. Thompson, Daniels lock horns over jobs: Frosty county reception for governor. In *Howey Politics Indiana* (January 31). www.howeypolitics.com

Innes, Judith, and Jane Rongerude. 2005. *Collaborative regional initiatives: Civic entrepreneurs work to fill the governance gap.* San Francisco: James Irvine Foundation.

Jensen, Merrill, ed. 1965. *Regionalism in America.* Madison: University of Wisconsin Press.

Karl, Herman A., Lawrence E. Susskind, and Katherine H. Wallace. 2007. A dialogue, not a diatribe: Effective integration of science and policy through joint fact finding. *Environment* 49: 20–34.

Keast, Robyn, Myrna P. Mandell, Kerry Brown, and Geoffrey Woolcock. 2004. Network structures: Working differently and changing expectations. *Public Administration Review* 64(3) (May/June): 363–371.

Keiter, Robert B. 1990. NEPA and the emerging concept of ecosystem management on the public lands. *Land and Water Law Review* 25(1): 43–60.

———. 1996. Toward legitimizing ecosystem management on the public domain. *Ecological Applications* 6(3): 727–730.

Kemmis, Daniel. 2001. *This sovereign land: A new vision for governing the west.* Washington, DC: Island Press.

Kenney, Douglas S. 1994. *Coordination mechanisms for the control of interstate water resources: A synthesis and review of the literature.* Boulder, CO: University of Colorado School of Law, Natural Resources Law Center, Advisory Commission on Intergovernmental Relations.

Kenney, Douglas, Sean T. McAllister, William H. Caile, and Jason S. Peckman. 2000. *The new watershed source book.* Boulder, CO: University of Colorado School of Law, Natural Resources Law Center.

Kitchen, Harry. 2003. Municipal restructuring: Are there lessons to be learned from the Canadian experience? Presented at the Institute for the Economy in Transition, Moscow, Russia, September 25.

Kwartler, Michael, and Gianni Longo. 2008. *Visioning and visualization: People, pixels, and plans.* Cambridge, MA: Lincoln Institute of Land Policy.

Leach, W. D. 2004. *Is devolution democratic? Assessing collaborative environmental management.* Sacramento: California State University, Center for Collaborative Policy.

Lee, Kai N. 1993. *Compass and gyroscope: Integrating science and politics for the environment.* Washington, DC: Island Press.

Lincoln Institute of Land Policy. 2009. www.lincolninst.edu/subcenters/regional-collaboration/

Little Hoover Commission. 2005. *Still imperiled, still important: The Little Hoover Commission's review of the CALFED Bay-Delta Program.* Sacramento, CA: Little Hoover Commission.

Lugar, Richard. 2005. Indianapolis can work better under consolidation plan. *Indianapolis Star* (January 3).

MacArthur Foundation. 2007. *Network on building resilient regions.* Chicago: John D. and Catherine T. MacArthur Foundation. www.macfound.org

Macfarlane, J., and B. Mayer. n.d. Evaluating environmental conflict resolution: Criteria identified in the literature. Tucson, AZ: U.S. Institute for Environmental Conflict Resolution.

MacGillis, Alec. 2006. More cooperation sought on area's future. *Washington Post* (June 21).

Mandell, Myrna P. n.d. The impact of changing expectations in complex networks. www.csus.edu/ccp/newsletter

Mathews, David. 2005. The politics of self-rule: Six public practices. *Connections* (Winter): 4–6.

McKinney, Matthew, and Kevin Essington. 2006. Learning to think and act like a region. *Land Lines* 18(1): 8–13.

McKinney, Matthew, and Patrick Field. 2005. Deliberative dialogue: From theory to practice. Missoula, MT: Public Policy Research Institute; Cambridge, MA: Consensus Building Institute.

————. 2008. Evaluating community-based collaboration on federal lands and resources. *Society and Natural Resources* 21: 419–429.

McKinney, Matthew, Patrick Field, and Shawn Johnson. 2007. Situation assessment report on terms of agreement for working together. (Prepared for Calgary Regional Partnership.) Missoula, MT: Public Policy Research Institute; Cambridge, MA: Consensus Building Institute.

McKinney, Matthew, and William Harmon. 2004. *The western confluence: A guide to governing natural resources.* Washington, DC: Island Press.

McKinney, Matthew, John Parr, and Ethan Seltzer. 2004. Working across boundaries: A framework for regional collaboration. *Land Lines* 16(3): 5–8.

Meck, Stewart, ed. 2002. The evolution of regional planning in the United States. In *Growing smart legislative guidebook.* Chicago: American Planning Association.

Meyer, William B., and Charles H. W. Foster. 2000. *New deal regionalism: A critical review.* Cambridge, MA: Harvard University, Kennedy School of Government.

Minister's Council on Municipal Sustainability 2007. Report to the Minister of Municipal Affairs. Alberta, CA: Minister of Municipal Affairs. www.assembly.ab.ca/lao/library/egovdocs/2007/alma/161349.pdf

National Association of Regional Councils. 2008. www.narc.org

Norgaard, R. B., and P. Baer. 2005. Collectively seeing complex systems: The nature of the problem. *Bioscience* (55)11: 953–960.

One Auckland Trust. 2008. Submission of the One Auckland Trust to the royal commission on Auckland governance. Auckland, New Zealand: One Auckland Trust.

Parr, John, Joan Riehm, and Christina McFarland. 2006. *Guide to successful local government collaboration in America's regions.* Washington, DC: National League of Cities.

Parr, John, Kim Walesh, and Chi Nguyen. 2002. *The practice of stewardship: Developing leadership for regional action.* Monograph Series 5. Mountain View, CA: Alliance for Regional Stewardship.

Peterson, Bart. 2005. *Indianapolis Works!* (September 19).

Peirce, Neal, and Curtis Johnson. 2000. Regional planning summit proceedings. *The Tennessean.*

PlaceMatters. 2008. www.placematters.com.

Porter, Douglas R., and Allan D. Wallis. 2002. *Exploring ad hoc regionalism.* Cambridge, MA: Lincoln Institute of Land Policy.

Powell, John Wesley. 1890. Institutions for the arid lands. *Century Magazine* (May–June): 111–116.

Quick, Larry. 2006. 21C placemaking: Creating place-based capability and value. South Melbourne, Australia: New Commons.

Quinn, Michael. 2006. Tools to map regional problems and opportunities. Presented at Regional Collaboration: Learning to Think and Act Like a Region, Seattle, WA (March 16).

Robbins, William G., Robert J. Frank, and Richard E. Ross, eds. 1983. *Regionalism and the Pacific Northwest.* Corvallis: Oregon State University Press.

Sale, Kirkpatrick. 2000. *Dwellers in the land: The bioregional vision.* Athens, GA: University of Georgia Press.

Schmidt, Lisa. 2007. Oilsands investment expected to surge. *Canada.com* (July 9).

Scholz, John T., and Bruce Stiftel, eds. 2005. *Adaptive governance and water conflict: New institutions for collaborative planning.* Washington, DC: Resources for the Future.

Snyder, Ken. 2006. Putting democracy front and center: Technology for citizen participation. *Planning* (July): 24–29.

Strong, Douglas. 1984. *Tahoe: An environmental history.* Lincoln: University of Nebraska Press.

Susskind, Lawrence. 1994. The need for a better balance between science and politics. In *Environmental diplomacy: Negotiating more effective global agreements.* New York: Oxford University Press.

Susskind, Lawrence, and Jeffrey Cruikshank. 1987. *Breaking the impasse: Consensual approaches to resolving public disputes.* New York: Basic Books.

———. 2006. *Breaking Robert's Rules: The new way to run your meeting, build consensus, and get results.* New York: Oxford University Press.

Susskind, Lawrence, Patrick Field, Mieke van der Wansem, and Jennifer Peyser. 2007. *Scientific information, stakeholder interests, and political concerns.* New York: Oxford University Press.

Susskind, Lawrence, and Merrick Hoben. 2004. Making regional policy dialogues work: A credo for metro-scale consensus building. *Temple Environmental Law & Technology Journal* 22(2): 123–138.

Susskind, Lawrence, Sarah McKearnan, and Jennifer Thomas-Larmer, eds. 1999. *The consensus building handbook: A comprehensive guide to reaching agreement.* Thousand Oaks, CA: Sage Publications.

Susskind, Lawrence, Mieke van der Wansem, and Armando Ciccarelli. 2008. A negotiation credo for controversial siting disputes. In *Multiparty negotiation,* eds. Lawrence Susskind and Larry Crump. Thousand Oaks, CA: Sage Publications.

U.S. EPA. 2000. *Projecting land-use change: A summary of models for assessing the effects of community growth and change on land-use patterns.* EPA/600/R-00/098. Cincinnati, OH: U.S. Environmental Protection Agency, Office of Research and Development.

U.S. FWS. 2005. Habitat conservation plans: Working together for endangered species. Washington, DC: U.S. Fish and Wildlife Service. www.fws.gov/endangered/pubs

University of Buffalo Regional Institute. 1999. *State of the region: Performance indicators for the Buffalo-Niagara region in the 21st century.* Buffalo, NY: University of Buffalo Regional Institute.

Weber, E. P. 2003. *Bringing society back in grassroots ecosystem management, accountability, and sustainable communities.* Cambridge, MA: MIT Press.

Western States Water Council. 1998. *State watershed strategy guidebook.* Midvale, UT: Western States Water Council.

White House Conference on Cooperative Conservation. 2005. St. Louis, August 29–31. http://cooperativeconservation.gov

Wondolleck, Julia, and Clare M. Ryan. 1999. What hat do I wear now? An examination of agency roles in collaborative processes. *Negotiation Journal* (April): 117–133.

Yaffee, Steven, Sheila Schueller, Stephen Higgs, Althea Dotzour, and Julia Wondolleck. 2003. *Measuring progress: An evaluation guide for ecosystem and community-based projects.* Ann Arbor: University of Michigan.

Yaffee, Steven L., Althea Dotzour, Stephen Higgs, Steven Hufnagel, Elizabeth McCance, Sheila Schueller, and Julia Wondolleck. 2004. *Measuring progress: A guide to the development, implementation, and interpretation of an evaluation plan.* Ann Arbor: University of Michigan, Ecosystem Management Initiative.

Index

Innes, Judith, 13
intergovernmental agreements (IGAs), 17–18
intergovernmental consolidations, 18–19
intermediary organizations, 20–21
intermunicipal development plans (IDPs),
    Calgary, 6–7
interviews, for situation assessment, 43–44
issues
    complexity and volatility, 40
    deliberation, 82–83
    leading to regional collaboration, 29, 35–39
    naming and framing, 81–82, 83–84
    situation assessment tool, 41–44
    See also process for solving issues

Jacksonville (FL), 19
Jefferson County (KY), 19, 137
Johnson, Curtis, 50
joint fact finding, 75–76, 77
joint services agreements, 18
Joint Venture: Silicon Valley Network (CA), 20, 64

key players, inclusion strategies, 56–57, 88–90
knowledge. *See* learning, scientific and public
    (principle 7)

land use
    Calgary, 6–7
    Envision Utah, 94–96
    partnerships and models, 14–19
    Portland, 132–133
    RPA and the Highlands, 96–98
leadership (principle 3), 30, 47–52
    capacity-building, 51–52
    characteristics, 47–49
    collaborative, 47–52
    roles, 49–50
    in sustained initiatives, 119
leadership institutes, 51–52
Leadership Middle Tennessee, 52
learn as you go (principle 10), 34, 107
    in principles of regional collaboration, 28,
        32–33
    See also evaluation
learning, scientific and public (principle 7), 31,
    75–84
    naming problems and framing options, 81–83
    political engagement, 83–84

tools for learning support, 76–80
Learning Network, 142
learning support tools, 76–80
legislation
    compacts, 15, 18
    coordination of jurisdictions, 21–22
    governance, 143
Lincoln Institute of Land Policy, 73, 76, 84,
    86, 142
Little Hoover Commission (CA), 100–101
long-term initiatives, 119–123
Louisville (KY), 19, 137
Lugar, Richard, 135–136, 137

Marion County (IN), 135–137
megaregions, 67–68
mergers, 19
Met Council (Minneapolis and St. Paul), 21,
    36–37, 56, 131–132
Metro (Portland, OR), 21, 132–133
Metro Vision 2020 (CO), 18, 129–130
metropolitan planning organizations
    (MPOs), 14
Mile High Compact (Denver), 18, 129–130
Minneapolis (MN), 21, 36–37, 56, 131–132
Minnesota legislature, 131–132
mobilization of people (principle 4), 30, 47,
    52–61
    building constituency, 53–54
    citizens' role, 57–61
    coalitions, 54–55
    decision makers, 55–56
    government participation, 57–59
    inclusion and alienation, 55
    inclusiveness, 53, 60
    key players, 56–57
    representation, 54–55
models. *See* governance models
Modesto (CA), 37
monitoring and measurement of progress, 107,
    109–110, 112, 118, 121
Montreal (QC), 19
Municipal Government Act (Calgary), 6–7
myregion.org (FL), 20, 38, 66

Nashville (TN), 50, 88
National Association of Regional Councils, 16
National Geographic Society (NGS), 38, 62, 64

About the Authors

Matthew J. McKinney is director of the Center for Natural Resources and Environmental Policy at The University of Montana, where he also serves as chair of the Natural Resources Conflict Resolution Program. He has more than 20 years of experience in collaboration and conflict resolution on a number of land use, natural resource, and environmental issues. He has professional affiliations with the Lincoln Institute of Land Policy, Consensus Building Institute, Rocky Mountain Land Use Institute, Association for Conflict Resolution, International Association for Public Participation, and American Planning Association. Contact: matt@cnrep.org

Shawn Johnson is an associate of the Center for Natural Resources and Environmental Policy at The University of Montana, where he focuses on cross-boundary land use, natural resource, and environmental policy challenges. He is also a doctoral student in natural resource policy and behavior at the University of Michigan's School of Natural Resources and Environment. His policy experience and training include a three-year stint as a legislative aide to U.S. Senator Max Baucus of Montana and a Master in Public Affairs degree from Princeton's Woodrow Wilson School. Contact: shawn@cnrep.org

About the Lincoln Institute of Land Policy

The Lincoln Institute of Land Policy is a private operating foundation whose mission is to improve the quality of public debate and decisions in the areas of land policy and land-related taxation in the United States and around the world. The Institute's goals are to integrate theory and practice to better shape land policy and to provide a nonpartisan forum for discussion of the multidisciplinary forces that influence public policy. This focus on land derives from the Institute's founding objective—to address the links between land policy and social and economic progress—that was identified and analyzed by political economist and author Henry George. The work of the Institute is organized in three departments: Valuation and Taxation, Planning and Urban Form, and International Studies. We seek to inform decision making through education, research, demonstration projects, and the dissemination of information through publications, our Web site, and other media. Our programs bring together scholars, practitioners, public officials, policy advisers, and involved citizens in a collegial learning environment. The Institute does not take a particular point of view, but rather serves as a catalyst to facilitate analysis and discussion of land use and taxation issues—to make a difference today and to help policy makers plan for tomorrow. The Lincoln Institute of Land Policy is an equal opportunity institution.

LINCOLN INSTITUTE
OF LAND POLICY

113 Brattle Street
Cambridge, MA 02138-3400 USA

Phone: 1-617-661-3016 x127 or 1-800-526-3873
Fax: 1-617-661-7235 or 1-800-526-3944
E-mail: help@lincolninst.edu
Web: www.lincolninst.edu